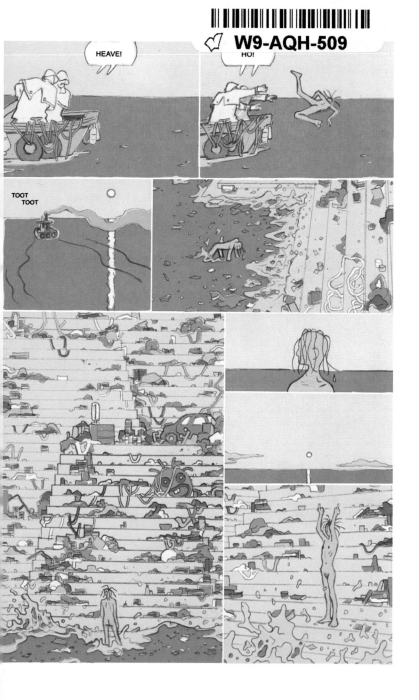

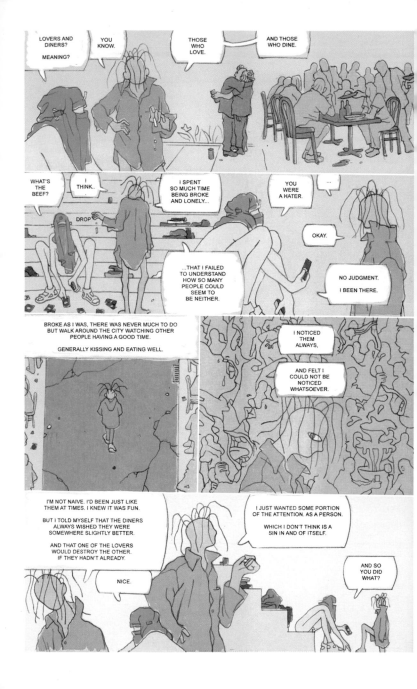

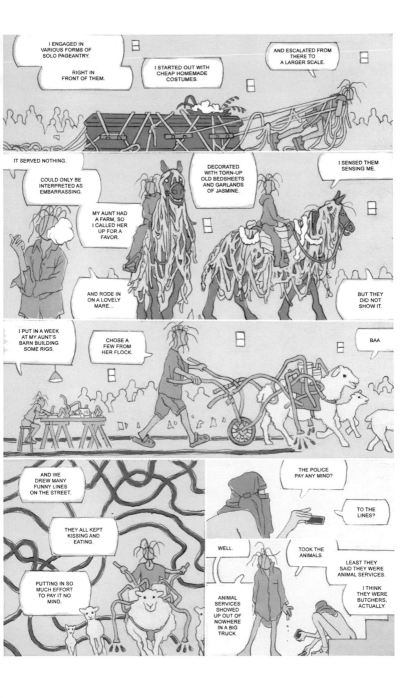

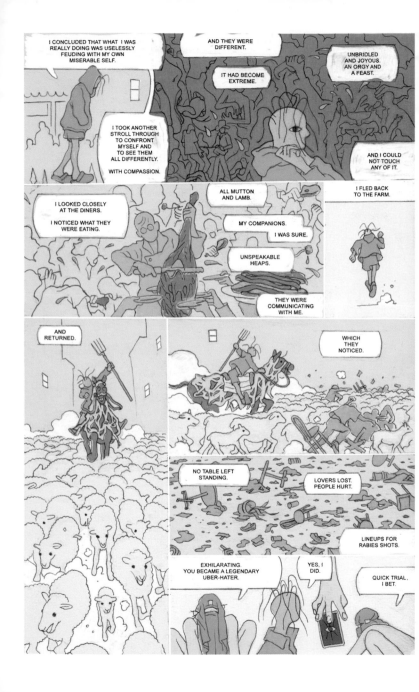

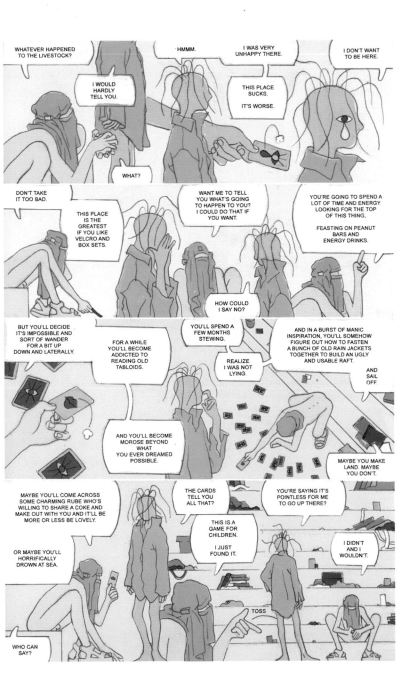

FOR DANIEL AND LISA

© 2022 McSweeney's Quarterly Concern and the contributors, San Francisco, California. ASSISTED BY: Annie Dills, Cameron Finch, Luke McCormick Gardiner, Ginger Greene, Julia Kornberg, Sophie Lalani, J. W. McCormack, Yasmin Patel, Alexander Rothstein, Noah Sneider, Maya Solovej, Raj Tawney, Tony Tulathimutte, Alvaro Villanueva, Abigail Walker, and Alex Woodend. COPY EDITOR: Caitlin Van Dusen. ASSOCIATE EDITOR: Lucy Huber. DIRECTOR OF SALES AND DISTRIBUTION: Dan Weiss. OPERATIONS MANAGER: Eric Cromie. TECHNOLOGY DIRECTOR: Nikky Southerland. ART DIRECTOR: Sunra Thompson. FOUNDING EDITOR: Dave Eggers. PUBLISHER & EXECUTIVE DIRECTOR: Amanda Uhle. EXECUTIVE EDITOR: Claire Boyle. VISITING EDITOR: James Yeh.

COVER ART: Benjamin Marra.

COVER LOGOTYPE: Phaedra Charles.

INTERIOR ILLUSTRATIONS: Jackie Ferrentino.

MCSWEENEY'S LITERARY ARTS FUND BOARD OF DIRECTORS: Natasha Boas, Carol Davis, Brian Dice (president), Isabel Duffy-Pinner, Caterina Fake, Hilary Kivitz, Jordan Kurland, Nion McEvoy, Gina Pell, Jeremy Radcliffe, Jed Repko, Vendela Vida.

Printed in the United States.

DEAR MCSWEENEY'S,
I am lying on my back in a
tent somewhere in British
Columbia, trying to keep my
thumbs warm as I peck this
out to you. My friend Helen
is six inches from me, rotat-
ing on her sleeping pad like
a kebab, occasionally clearing
the phlegm from her throat.
We don't say good morning
to each other, and we don't
say good night. We treat each
other like soldiers, united by
our singular mission: we are
bicycling from Key West,
Florida, to the arctic pipeline
town of Deadhorse, Alaska.

When people inquire about
our greatest hardships, many
guess grizzly bears, moose,
or steep mountains, while
others conjure up images of
sinister men carrying knives
and lurking outside our tent.
The truth, however, is that our
greatest enemy has been far
sneakier, and invisible to the
naked eye: the wind.

It began in Florida as
a steady gale, but it was
manageable. Then it picked
up in Arkansas, building into
a large roar. By the time we

reached Oklahoma, it was a
full-blown terror.

In the vast stretches
of prairie between towns,
pushing your way through the
stubborn air, you feel as if you
are at sea. The wind crashes
against you like waves—
building, building, and then
manifesting in a massive gust.
It disorients and nauseates,
and it has a sound—a relent-
less, deafening howl.

For the most part, the
winds come from the side,
blowing from the south as we
bike west. They have battered
our left sides for hundreds of
miles, eroding layers of skin.
When I talk to people, I expect
them to comment that my face
looks like the side of a jagged
mountain. In these side winds,
you learn to surf each gust, as
if riding a wave, leaning your
body against its perceived
edge. The trick is to predict
the moment the gust will
end, righting your handlebars
a moment before so that you
don't tip over.

To cope, you have to
burrow somewhere deep
inside yourself, numb your

mind—make yourself into something more animal. Before the trip, I had hoped to have deep and complex reflections, maybe even a personal revelation. Instead, my thoughts have boiled down to the simplest of prayers: that the road might change direction, or that a line of trees might briefly block the gusts. Another common escape fantasy is visualizing myself walking from my apartment to the coffee shop and ordering an iced coffee. For strength, I chant my boyfriend's nickname. Other times, I make up verses to a song called "Everyone in the World Is Dead." And when I really need to transcend my physical reality, I shove earplugs into my ears, put on bone-vibrating headphones, and blast Chopin at full volume, imagining my circumstance as a scene in a black-and-white film in the Criterion Collection.

It's one thing to suffer in isolation, but as you're bicycling, people blast by you in the comfort of their windless automotive pods. It's humiliating to be observed through windows, like an animal in a zoo, as you engage in what feels like the struggle of a lifetime. You're barely moving, they see your suffering, and yet they do nothing to help.

Gas stations have become my only respite, and their employees the gatekeepers between the two worlds: the wind and the not-wind. I enter, dazed and relieved, like a drunken sailor returned to shore. The employees and I make eye contact. "The wind," I tell them. "The wind is really bad."

Friends of the bike trip nod; enemies stare at me blankly. Then I find a corner to slump down in, close my eyes, and enjoy the ordered and obedient air. How nicely it hangs there! It's still enough to hear the quiet hum of the refrigerators, and I can feel my face again. When I open my eyes, I'm satisfied that the objects in the room are exactly as I left them, the Twinkies and Ding Dongs all in their place.

My one point of pride, after all this battling, is that I've become a bit of a wind connoisseur. When I feel it on my face, I breathe it in, and I can identify the speed of the gale. In a twenty-mile-per-hour gust, you know to hold on, but at thirty you feel afraid. That's when stop signs rattle off their hinges, roofs fly off houses, and porta-potties tip onto their sides. Once, at a rest stop, I scooped a handful of peanuts from my bag and they took flight from my palm, scattering like birds.

Around Wyoming, I experienced the wind in fleeting psychedelic moments. One day in the midst of my struggle, I looked up and saw the other creatures that live in the wind. There were cattle, sheep, and mountain goats huddled together behind trees and small mounds. Mother cows blocked the wind, shielding their calves. Beautiful creatures that stand in this wind with me, I thought, I am sympathetic to all of you! I blessed every man and beast that has stood in this wind:

blessed the woolly mammoths, arctic foxes, early settlers, Indigenous people, Lewis and Clark's forgotten helpers, marching armies. Perhaps we were made from the same fabric of God!

But most days wrestling the wind feels like defying a divine order. Is there some nobility, some meaning in this? Am I like Jacob's angel, proving my faith in some monumental struggle? Or am I a fool, out here day after day, for no reason other than that I said I would be?

I often want to give up, very badly. I want to fly to the people who actually love me, who want to hold me, rather than battle the invisible hand of God. Grappling with the wind is a pointless endeavor, maybe the way life is a point-less endeavor. One in which challenges push against you at random, and you struggle against them, and then, for no reason, they disappear.

Fighting the steady gales,

BIANCA GIAEVER

KOOTENAY NATIONAL PARK,
BC, CANADA

DEAR MCSWEENEY'S,
I write this letter to you on the day of the week widely recognized as "Tuesday."

Of the "Seven Major Days"—that age-old consortium of days that together provides the basic structure of our calendar week—Tuesday seems to have the most tenuous hold on the popular imagination and the culture at large. Take this excerpt from Chris Rock's opening monologue on *Saturday Night Live*, performed on October 3, 2020:

> The government does not want you to vote. Why do I know [that]? Because Election Day is a *Tuesday in November*. Why? Anybody here ever put something on a Tuesday in November? Does anybody get married on a Tuesday in November? Church ain't on a Tuesday. Even Jesus avoids Tuesday. You know, if this show was *Tuesday Night Live*, it would have got canceled in 1975.

In Mr. Rock's telling, Tuesday is such a nonevent that it undermines democracy, and, if given a chance, would wreak similar havoc on the domains of matrimony, religion, and entertainment. While played to comic effect on the show, his charges are nonetheless serious and deserving of deep consideration. Indeed, given the current social climate of reappraising long-standing cultural traditions and advocating for necessary structural changes, it would seem the time is ripe to reckon with the legacy of the temporal institution known as "Tuesday."

Tuesday first came to my attention as a young person growing up in the Dallas–Fort Worth metroplex. Exactly how I came to know of it, I cannot say. I can say, however, that I have no recollection of *not* knowing it (or any of the other days of the week, for that matter), so I must have been very young. A child, even.

The strict Monday-through-Friday regimen

I adhered to for my schooling from pre-K onward instilled in me a set of associations for each day of the week—with the notable exception of Tuesday. Monday was slightly dreaded, as it marked the start of the week. Wednesday was like reaching the peak of a hard-to-climb mountain. Thursday had the ease of climbing down said mountain. Friday carried a joyous feeling of release. Saturday held the promise of exploration and fun. Sunday was often quieter and more leisurely. Tuesday? Just kind of there.

The human race has certainly tried to make something out of Tuesday over the years, with varying results. The NFL has attempted to play football games on Tuesdays, but for some reason has done so only ten times in its more than one-hundred-year history. America declared its independence from England on a Tuesday, but the founders proved unable to turn that into a regular weekly thing. The most successful attempt to make meaning out of Tuesday is perhaps Taco Tuesday, a widespread practice of offering deals for tacos on Tuesdays, reportedly pioneered by a Wyoming-based chain called Taco John's. While Taco Tuesday has been comparatively successful, does it elevate Tuesday's stature enough to meet the challenges laid out by Mr. Rock? I'm not so sure.

I don't have any hard-and-fast solutions for Tuesday. Perhaps the day will come when Tuesday is deemed too inefficient a day to exist, too outdated a day to meet the exigencies of the twenty-first century. But I will offer this observation: while Tuesday may not have a single, powerful, centralized association, it does seem malleable enough to take on many different associations. Individually, those associations don't command much respect, but if they were united under one umbrella, then perhaps Tuesday could hold its own among the other days of the week. People are fond of saying "TGIF"—"Thank God It's Friday"—on Friday. Maybe on Tuesday they could say "TTBD"—"Tuesday: To Be Determined"—a neologism that would embrace Tuesday's open-ended nature and encourage people to generate their own meanings for the day.

"TTBD"—try dropping it into your everyday conversations and let me know how it goes.

Until next time,

IKECHUKWU UFOMADU
BROOKLYN, NY

DEAR MCSWEENEY'S,
I have "writer's block." I tried to explain this condition—that I am unable to do WRITING, in the professional sense—but the letter got pretty long and complicated, and I decided to transfer it to one of my journals to expand on it. These days I keep three journals: one in which I write in the morning, by hand, usually sitting up in bed; one on the computer, which I first began as a warm-up to WRITING (back when I used to do it); and another, newer one called my "gratitude" journal, where I record only "positive" things, to train my brain to focus not only on problems, of which the other journals pretty much entirely consist.

The problem is that I tend to make everything a problem, and even when something is not a problem but material for the gratitude journal, I turn *that* into a problem by being unable to just accept it as a gift.

For example, the fiction class I taught this semester went so well that my gratitude about it turned to unease. The students had such fantastic chemistry with one another, making jokes and witticisms at just the right moments, that it seemed they could've been performing a stand-up routine—"I'm in love with all of you," one finally quipped in the middle of class, and then blushed. The stories I'd randomly assigned for workshop each day were often weirdly thematically linked, so much so that I began to suspect a supernatural influence. Had God/the Universe conspired to put these twenty-one people together in a room? To believe this was happening—amid war, a pandemic, a multitude of divorces, and other, smaller atrocities—also created a sense of reproach in me, that I would think such a thing.

Another example, an experience with a Whole Fruit coconut ice pop that I had after a long walk through the neighborhood the other night: Why had it tasted so startlingly delicious, as if I had never tasted an ice pop before? And what did it mean to experience the taste of coconut after not having noted the taste of anything in weeks? I hadn't bought the ice pop myself, and this, too, seemed important—that it had been left in the freezer nearly a year ago by the owner of the house. Why had I, at that moment, finally desired something

I'd overlooked for nearly a year, something I'd never have bought myself? Had it not been warm outside that night, and had I not been out of lime seltzer, I'd never even have thought of the ice pop. I couldn't help but have a sense of foreboding about the whole thing, about how it had almost not been.

Then the sex with X the other day at his house after my having been celibate for a year. Was it the seeming rightness of the connection with him, or some inner shift that allowed me to connect with him that afternoon? And were such decisions "real," as in true decisions, or simply responses to a long chain of preparatory events from the universe that causes us, in a moment, to "answer" one way or the other?

I do edit out the problem-centric aspects of what I note in the gratitude journal, and I've learned that when writing in it, I should also have open my "regular" journal so that I can go back and forth, noting the subject matter one way in the gratitude journal and then going over it in a different way in the other journal—the regular computer journal and the notebook journal both being free of constraint.

It was this *lack of constraint* that once excited me, when, years ago, I first began keeping these journals—much in the same way that it is the *constraint* of the gratitude journal that now compels me—and I recall the perverse satisfaction of writing in them what I imagined would bore other people, a response to the pressure of being a WRITER, which meant writing what is *interesting*, the subtext being interesting to *both* me and an audience—a compromise— and I wished to end the sense of an audience in my head, in my being.

I then spent some years in dialogue with myself, learning to become my own audience, to surprise myself with confessions and advice that seemed both to come and not to come from me. This was not a writer's trick—to self-consciously shed self-consciousness to produce publishable writing—but a true attempt at *nonachievement*. I mean, my goal was to write nothing readable (and certainly nothing salable) for another human being, to write not exactly badly but not well, to write *beyond* badly and well—which began not long after a therapist diagnosed me as being "disconnected" from myself, whatever that means.

I do suppose that when I become "reconnected" to myself I may stop keeping three journals, which have succeeded in not being fake writer-y journals. I mean, they are not veiled novels or memoirs. There are no hopes that they will one day be read and appreciated, but rather my brother has promised he will destroy everything once I am dead.

Certainly I think the way we think of "writer's block" should be changed. Because I have had it awhile now and the notebook journals have accumulated into a sort of tower that threatens to topple over, which pleases me and even has that pleasurable edge of having been done *against* someone, though I have not been able to decide for sure who that person is. (No doubt, reading this, you have a theory; of course I've thought of that myself.)

I do hope I may be coming close to connecting with myself and that the writer's block will soon end. I intuit that mastering the gratitude journal may be the last step. Until then I am able only to write in the journals and write letters to friends—I am able to write this now only because I am writing to you—and currently remain trapped inside the addiction and pleasure and torment of NON-WRITING, which I do recommend.

Warmest, and with gratitude,

APRIL AYERS LAWSON
GREENVILLE, SC

DEAR MCSWEENEY'S,
The other day, the comedy writer Jessi Klein was on *Fresh Air*, relaying how, immediately after giving birth, she'd looked down at her belly and noted that her skin had the same goose-pimply, leathery texture as a deflated basketball. Fascinating! I thought. Would that happen to me too? Pregnancy was turning out to be the weirdest thing I had ever experienced, and I was continually shocked by its bizarre symptoms. Something was always going on.

One night, for instance, after taking a shower, I looked in the mirror and saw something glistening, organ-like, poking out of my belly button. Was that my intestine?! I knew that during pregnancy, innies often became outies, and belly buttons could disappear altogether. But this quivering mass resembled a mollusk that was being evicted from its too-small hiding place. I summoned my spouse into the bathroom and said very quietly, "My belly is stretched so tight I think it's literally burst." He wanted to touch the shiny tissue with a Q-tip, and I screamed, not knowing whether it would hurt. "Have you ever seen the end of your belly button?" he asked. No. My belly button had always been so deep that ever since I was a child, I'd worried that if I stuck my finger in there, I'd touch the other side. This was only confirming my suspicions that I had never been enclosed properly. Long story short: we gently scraped away the mass with an alcohol-soaked swab, which eventually revealed a hard, stony cap underneath, not unlike an operculum. A navel stone! This was what googling led us to conclude. It appeared I had always possessed this humble belly jewel, and I'd never known it.

Every day of pregnancy was an adventure. Early on, I developed a hyper-specific, police-dog-caliber sense of smell that made every walk up our stairwell a forensic accounting of what the neighbors had eaten for lunch, among their other activities. At first this was fun, but soon every smell, pleasant or unpleasant, triggered waves of debilitating nausea. If I bent down too far, I would throw up in my mouth, then accidentally snort up the vomit and choke on it—a common occurrence. In my second trimester, an angry boob rash stampeded across my chest, a virally-induced affliction that commonly plagues pregnant people because of our weakened immune systems. (Pregnancy, I learned, suppresses immunity so your body won't reject the alien creature growing inside your uterus.) Later, on the cusp of my third trimester, my ass—apparently crushed by my own weight from sitting, the way a beached whale crushes itself with its own blubber—began to hurt. My spouse pulled up a mirror so I could see: a bloom of pink and purple welts, like the aftermath of an overzealous BDSM spanking session.

Friends often asked how I was doing as we strolled at a glacial pace around the park, the only pace I could maintain without losing my breath. (My lungs were now squished-flat pancakes that struggled to oxygenate twice the normal volume of blood.) Even though I am what medical professionals call a "geriatric" mom, I am still an outlier among my close cohort of artists and academics, who either don't want children or can't envision children, due to their undersized apartments and oversize student loans. I always played up the drama so nobody would feel any FOMO. "Well, last week I went to the doctor to check out this antler thing growing out of my right nipple," I reported one day. "It looked like a piece of coral. I thought it was some kind of nipple herpes. The OB took one look, twiddled it for a second, and said it was completely normal, a skin tag." But did I have to get it removed? "Only if the baby started chewing on it and it bothered me." Luckily the thing shriveled up and fell off on its own.

So, I learned pregnant people got skin tags, and it was normal, the way all those other phenomena were normal too. The hair emerging in weird places, the bloody gums, the teeth chipping, et cetera. I wondered how someone in the Dark Ages would have experienced their symptoms without the encyclopedic guidance of Reddit forums. During Victorian times, women even wore—horrifyingly—pregnancy corsets. Now that's a head-in-the-sand kind of garment. I guess the whole process of pregnancy was so scary that it was better to pretend it wasn't happening. With each new thing I googled, I became more and more grateful for modern science and medicine and to be alive in the twenty-first century. As scary as things got, it was always just a hormone thing, and hormones were the magical potions, catalyzing miraculous, Ovid-worthy transformations. Hormones caused your feet to stretch, your hip ligaments to loosen and wobble, your fingers to bloat so dramatically your wedding ring threatened amputation. They caused your boobs to leak as though you'd just thrown a shirt on over a wet swimsuit. They instructed your baby to grow the placenta, that incredible, bloody, life-giving organ that now fed him. Hormones directed the whole show.

I wondered: Were hormones to blame for my recent catastrophizing, my inability to see hope on the horizon? In May 2022, I read headlines about the likely overturn of *Roe v. Wade*, and how some states were already gearing up to outlaw abortion without exceptions for rape or incest. You feel yourself shrink to pellet-size. You see on your phone a photo of an abortion-rights rally, where young women are carrying signs that depict a red *X* over a clothes hanger. *A clothes hanger.* Is this where we are again? Because the conservative supermajority in the Supreme Court has decided that pregnant people aren't dealing with enough, haven't been punished enough. You read about the

consequences of abortion bans already playing out in Poland, where a young mother died because doctors were afraid to terminate her abnormal fetus before saving her. "A woman is like an incubator," she said in one of her last texts to her family. Now that you're experiencing motherhood firsthand, you understand in a visceral way how terrifying it must be to have to terminate a pregnancy, and how much more terrifying it must be to have no options. You try to imagine hauling yourself to work while sore, bloated, underpaid, unsupported, forced to bring to term a baby whose father abuses you. You try to unsee a vision of a desperate woman beating her own belly or throwing herself down the stairs. As foggy as my brain has become, I can still wrap my head around a lot: I can get behind the neural pruning and the dissolving of my brain's gray matter. But I don't think I'll ever be able to comprehend the hearts and minds of religious fanatics who want to take us back to the Dark Ages. No amount of brain plasticity, or hormonal magic, will ever get me to see that point of view.

Yours,

ANELISE CHEN
NEW HAVEN, CT

DEAR MCSWEENEY'S,

I'm a bad liar, which doesn't necessarily make me a natural or capable truth-teller. I want to ask you: Between reality and imagination, which has felt more within arm's reach these days? Some days, I have the disconcerting sense that I've offered neither a good truth nor a good lie to the world. I wonder about those days—days when the territories of truth and falsehood feel similarly gated off, leaving us to idle in some other, in-between place.

I lied the other day, badly, to my landlord. Weeks before, a fist-sized hole appeared in our living room window. Its origins, at first, were mystifying: it looked as though something had been thrown through the window,

but there was no object to be found amid the collection of glass fragments on the hardwood floor. There was no loud sound to be remembered, no video footage to be reviewed, no discernible motive to serve as pretense (my roommate and I considered and ruled out a list of people who had varying and justifiable reasons to dislike us—each seemed like someone who'd consider themself above inflicting property damage).

Weeks later, my landlord came to insert a new pane. I looked at him with a manufactured cluelessness. "It's so weird," I offered. "I still don't understand what could've happened."

"Well, I've seen weirder things happen in this apartment," he said, as though to reassure us. And that was that.

But I'd discovered, in the month or so it'd taken him to remedy the hole, its origins: BLT. BLT, our ten-year-old neighbor, who lives in a house without other children, who is restlessly lonely, who knocks on our door most days after school to see if we're free to play Frisbee. It was a crime, in a sense, of love. BLT came clean to my roommate a few days after it happened: he'd knocked on our window over and over again that afternoon, with whatever quantity of fevered passion is sufficient to eventually break glass. Neither of us had been home.

BLT is a nickname, not a pseudonym. We'd given one another nicknames the day we'd first met, markers of our burgeoning friendship. We told him he'd be BLT—his initials are LT, and we decided the *B* could stand for *big* (though he wasn't large in any sense). He gave my roommate the nickname Captain Sparkle, for his buoyant disposition. He nicknamed me Tomorrow, because it sounded, to him, like Ricardo. When spring came, we fell into the habit of occasionally spending time together, usually during the unregulated hours between 5:00 and 7:00 p.m., after school or work but before

dinner—a difficult time for ten-year-old boys and twenty-six-year-old boys, when idleness threatens to poke awake our most unappeasable thoughts. We throw my roommate's Frisbee on the small patch of concrete in front of our apartment. We tell BLT about our jobs, our families, our lives before we came to Oakland. BLT tells us about his dogs, his crush, the unrelenting social dramas of fifth grade. "There are real broskis and fake broskis, and you have to know the difference!" he warns, giving several allegories, instances of unforgivable betrayals between boys, to substantiate his argument. "Fake broskis mess you up. Real broskis save your life."

I guess I envy the way BLT holds his loneliness, the damage he's willing to risk in its name. I moved to the West Coast in the winter of the pandemic. I left behind friends, parents, a nascent love, an old dream. I've poured my heart into my job—as a case manager at a

high school in Oakland—
which I hardly ever feel like
I'm doing justice to. I grow
fearful I am being perma-
nently recalibrated, somehow,
by my loneliness. Recently,
more and more older people
in my life have been attempt-
ing to reassure me; they
promise me I'll be able to
metabolize the hardships of
these years into the material
needed for a good future life.
They promise me that things
get better, that any suffering
at this age becomes justified
over time. Their statements
feel like good lies, useful ones
for us both to believe.

I felt guilty, watching
my landlord work on his
knees while I read a book
in our living room. He's a
sweet guy, with an adorable
one-eyed dog. He is fixing
someone else's damage. He
must be able to tell that
I know what happened.
I consider fessing up, but
I catch myself—I have to act
like a real broski. Apart from
owning an East Oakland
triplex, my landlord works
on films; he told me he

worked on the production
team of *An Inconvenient Sequel:
Truth to Power*, a lesser-known
follow-up to Al Gore's *An
Inconvenient Truth.* Al Gore
probably pays good, I think.
And my landlord, how-
ever kind, has indisputably
profiteered from Bay Area
gentrification. In tandem,
these thoughts successfully
eliminate my guilt.

I want to share with
BLT two lines from a Louise
Glück poem: "We look at the
world once, in childhood. /
The rest is memory." I have
a sense that, were he really
to comprehend these lines,
every detail and ache in his
mercurial life would appear
beautiful. In understanding
the lines, maybe he could love
his loneliness, come to regard
it as its own consolation. But
I know, without telling him,
that he won't understand.
What does childhood mean,
after all, to a child? It is a
name, like most names, that
defines something seen from
some sufficient distance;
only when we lack childhood
do we come to make sense

of its nature; in its sudden absence, we assign it meaning, and a discernible place in the landscape of language. Love, citizenship, authority, childhood: ask first the people who've lost these things, or else those who've never possessed them in the first place, to tell you their true meanings. Plus, I don't want to become just like those older advice-givers, believing themselves able to carry solace across the chasm of experience; it's a fool's errand, in the end, to feign the shape of another's tomorrow.

I should be more generous in my time with BLT. I hope I'll spend some summer afternoons in his company, throwing the Frisbee, exchanging chatter or silence, fending off something together.

Abrazos,

RICARDO FRASSO
JARAMILLO
OAKLAND, CA

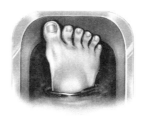

THE NEW TOE

by ZACH WILLIAMS

I WAS ON THE lidded toilet, head in hand, when my two-year-old spun around in the tub, leaned back, raised his legs from the water, and planted both feet on the tiled wall to reveal, there on his left foot, a new toe. There was no mistaking it. You wouldn't have had to count.

Buddy, I said, your foot—

But he spun again, sat up, filled the blue whale pitcher with water, and poured it onto the bath mat. I said, No—water stays in the tub. *Why?* he asked, and I said, Because it makes a mess, that's why, you know why.

Now he sat with the left foot tucked under him. I rolled up my sleeve and said, Pal, come here a sec. He squirmed away, shouting, *You can't!* Real quick, I said, then grabbed hold of the foot and pulled it from the tepid water. There it was. The new toe, slippery and delicate as the others, sat crowded between the fourth toe and what should have been the fifth.

You have to pay attention to moments like that. Something, all at once, where before there was nothing. I had the sense of being in two different places: on the toilet at bath time, yes, but also at a point of departure. We were entering a zone of genuine possibility.

Then I said, Hey, stop, don't drink that. He'd been pretending to sip from the whale pitcher and now finally he'd done it. *Why?* he asked. Because, I said, you peed in that water. He drank again.

I rolled my neck to crack its joints, bit my cheeks, tried to think.

A new toe like that—what could explain it? It was important to come to some understanding there. Because I would have to tell people—the pediatrician, his day care—and in doing so, I'd be made to account for the toe. I would be answerable to it, as I was answerable to every aspect of his life, as a steward of his growth and good health and general success as an organism. And the toe had only just appeared, out of the blue; I knew next to nothing about it. As a birth defect, of course, it might have been perfectly ordinary. But I didn't have the luxury of such a clear-cut explanation. I thought back to the moment, before the bath, when I'd peeled his orange socks off. If the toe had been there, I certainly would have noticed. True, I was exhausted—he'd been up multiple times every night that week—and maybe I wasn't the best or most reliable observer. But I felt sure there'd been no new toe before the tub. And if that was right, then the toe was less than fifteen minutes old.

It must have just sprouted.

I squeezed the baby wash into my hand. Time for soap, I said, and he yelled, *No soap!*

But then, I thought, rubbing down his chest and struggling arms, that couldn't be. Because who had ever heard of such a thing? No one. By any conventional measure, it was impossible, and even putting that aside, there were logical issues here. For example, you'd think he'd have felt it shooting up and out of his little foot. I tried to imagine the sensation—painful, or itchy, or startling, anyway. And yet there he was, in the water, playing now with his pirate ship, without a care in the world. Besides, if he'd really sprouted a new toe, then why should that be the end of it? The rules had changed, in that case. We were now in a sprouted-toe world, and the door was open to all kinds of wacky shit: toes all over his body, sudden extra toes on, say, ten other children from around the world, and together they would have to, I don't know, do something extraordinary one day. I looked up at the closed bathroom door. A white towel hung there on a hook. It might be weirder. The toe might be the least of our concerns. If it really had sprouted, then beyond that door might be a set of conditions so startling that the instant we stepped out, we'd forget all about the toe. We could be floating in space, for all I knew, just a bathroom in a void.

I leaned over on the toilet, opened the door, peered out. No void.

Then I filled the whale pitcher, shook loose the plastic Grover that had gotten swept inside, rinsed the soap from his body, rubbing his back with my palm. Well, I decided, I was wrong, then. I had to be. Because the idea of the toe was unassimilable. And that meant that the problem wasn't with his foot. The problem was with me. I was mistaken. Overtired, depressed, bored. I pressed the heels of my hands into my eyes until I saw colors. He opened and closed the drain repeatedly. The new toe was not possible. Therefore, the new toe did not exist. I blinked, stared at it. I touched it again.

But it couldn't be real. And so it wasn't. Simple as that.

I poured the pitcher over his head, shampooed his hair, rinsed it out. And I thought, Okay, look. If the toe were both there and not there, then it would be, it would have to be, subject to a different kind of approach. It might be *real*, but not physically real—*there*, but not literally there. Aloud, to no one, I muttered, Hear me out. He arched rudely against the floor of the tub and said, *I'm pressing my penis!* Imagine a third path, between here and not-here. You might start down that third path like this: Why a toe? Like, of all things, why that? What's connoted by a toe? Yes, this seemed exciting, this seemed fruitful, and I thought, Well, toes are agents of balance, offering supple points of connection to the ground. Toes are flexible. They grasp. Toes operate as a collective; they—

Crash you! he shouted, slamming his pirate ship down onto the water. My pants got all wet. And, toweling myself off, I thought, No, that's not fruitful; it's idiotic. It was a toe, a real toe, now breaching the yellow water, beside the rubber octopus. It was no figment. We were right back to sprouted. And why did that feel so awful? Because, somehow or other, I guessed I'd fucked up. I *would* have to call the pediatrician, and the day care, and others, many others. They'd want to know about the moment I'd noticed it. There would be questions about the delay that was, even now, growing between that moment and the first instance, whatever it was to be, of assertive parental action on my part. Hang on, they'd all say. You thought it might be "fruitful" to try a "nonliteral" approach?

Then I looked up and gasped: Whoa, whoa, buddy, stop stop stop *stop*!

He was trying to climb out. He had all his weight on the left foot, six toes and all, and was tottering on the lip. *Ready for big bed!* he announced, and just as he began to fall I scooped him up. I pressed him to me, pulled the towel from the door, kissed his wet head. He was such a beautiful boy. I loved him to death. I carried him out, dropped him giggling onto the bed, smiled down at him. The poor little thing.

Trains or dinos, I asked, meaning PJs, and he said, *Trains!* I reached down and took hold of the foot, bent close, peered at the toe, looked up at his face. Then I took the toe between my thumb and forefinger. This little piggy, I said, and twisted it hard to the right. He shrieked and rolled away, looked up at me with real hurt in his eyes. Kiss it, make it better? I asked, and he nodded. I bent my lips to the extra toe. This was all so horrible. I hated myself, hated being myself.

Wait here, bud, I said.

In the cupboard above the sink was the baby Benadryl. I drew a dose into the plastic syringe. Then I opened the Tupperware with all the weed stuff and dug around for the gummies. Last, under the sink, the rubber bands and wire cutters.

Special dessert? he said, eyes wide.

Special dessert, I said, and he snatched the gummy—*Spe-ci-al desserrrrt!*—and ate it up.

Now sleepy juice.

Like a little bird, he opened his mouth for the syringe.

And tonight, I told him, you get to read as many books as you want.

Ma and Pa Pickles are going on a picnic. Here comes Ma with the picnic basket. Please hurry up, Ma! He lay on my chest, moving his whole head to take in the pictures. In their convertible, the happy pigs drove through town and onto the highway, past a work site—*Excavator*, he said, pointing—and up the icy mountain, where the watermelon truck lost its load, and then down to the beach, and the Pickles family ate and bathed and sunned together. I felt jealous of them, the Pickleses, in their sprawling, well-manicured scenario.

By the time I closed the book, he was heavy and still.

Buddy? I said, and let him roll onto the bed—white as milk, the right eye closed more than the left. He'll be fine, I said aloud, and kept saying it, bunching the towel under his left ankle, rolling the train pajamas to the knee, cinching the thickest rubber bands around the foot's middle.

Buddy, I said. Hey, buddy. I took up the wire cutters. Hey. Buddy.

Just a trace of blood and a bit of hollow bone, like a quill.

See, I said. It was hardly anything in the first place. No problem.

But I wasn't feeling so hot. I rolled the toe in tissues and flushed it down the toilet. And then I bundled his left foot in five socks: two Batman, two bananas, one Elmo. I picked him up, stood swaying with him in my arms, saying, You're okay, you're okay, and then I turned out the lights and lowered him into the crib. Felt glad it was too dark to see. Reached out again, the crib was gone. Then the floor went. Now do me, please, I said, falling already, and as I fell, I thought, Oh, my fucking god, yes, yes, here it comes—

ASYMPTOTE

by SIQI LIU

WHEN PHIL COLLINS SHOWED up on our patio two years after he'd escaped from his tank, my mother said, "The year I was in Yunnan—I don't know if I've ever told you about it. That year I tasted so much bitterness. Suan la, I'll tell you later— anyway, that year I ate quite a few turtles."

"How?" I was usually embarrassed by my mother's tendency to share things that were bizarre and intimate, but this time I was curious about the inevitable.

"Very easy. We'd stick a chopstick in front of the turtle's mouth, wait for it to bite down, pull the chopstick backward until its neck gets stretched out, then quickly chop off its head. We'd slice through its stomach and wash it clean. We'd eat it with white pepper. We'd eat it with the shell. This is what you do for the shell: Only the middle part is hard, like a bone, and the rest of it is very soft, like the edges of a skirt. The whole thing can be sliced into maybe seven portions, and each person gets to eat one portion. Sometimes there are eggs inside the turtle—you can eat that too. The bone is used for medicine. After the bone dries out, you can light it like a candle, and it will drive away mosquitoes."

Now my mother is holding a chopstick in one hand, a cleaver in another. Light dances on its silver edge each time she flicks her wrist, rehearsing the motion in midair. Phil Collins regards the knife, blinking his glassy brown eyes lazily, unmoving. He looks just as catatonic as he did two years ago, when his escape astounded all of us (summer twilight, the front door ajar, a trail of water dribbled across our living room carpet). Before he opens his mouth, before he clamps down on the wood,

I go back into the house. We have turtle soup that night, garnished with herbs we've been growing on our windowsill. The first real protein we've had in weeks.

Last spring, not long after my father died, I took up the habit of driving out to the snow-laden cornfields after school—sometimes with Rick or Dana, sometimes alone. I was with Dana the first twilight when it appeared next to the moon, a red smudge on the horizon I could blot out with my thumb. By the time I got home, there were men in suits getting interviewed on TV, pointing at white graphs on which the smudge lingered like a wine stain. The men used increasingly ominous phrases like "devastating impact" and "nongravitational force" until my mother clicked off the TV. She had done this often during fights with my father. She seemed to revel in her ability to toss the colorful images on-screen into a dark void, the sheer efficiency of that destruction. "Go do your homework," she said.

At first things went on as normal. My mother went to work at the senior center for Taiwanese

American grandparents whose children were busy at work. There she wiped the spit off their chins, played ping-pong with the sprightlier ones. I went to school, where teachers were assigning us less homework than usual—an early sign of trouble, we should've known. But I was preoccupied with the rumors that I had lost my virginity to Carl, a stumpy, freckled boy who was said to have weird toes. Within a couple of weeks, though, none of that mattered. School closed; grocery stores were raided. The precarity of our invisible supply chain was revealed ("But I thought this was all *automated*," Dana wailed over the phone in those early days, bemoaning her delayed shipments of eczema treatment). The red smudge took on a rounder shape.

Today is Wednesday, garbage day. I sort the trash and the recycling into separate bins the way my father taught me and wheel them to the end of our driveway. White bags are strewn along our street like piles of snow that refuse to melt, and the air stinks of rotten banana peels and stale blood. But since our neighbors are still wheeling their bins out, I decide it is best to follow suit.

"The grass has gotten very tall," I report to my mother. She is standing in front of our fridge door, contemplating the bulleted items on her magnetic dry-erase board. "Should I mow the lawn?"

"What's the use?" She is uninterested, doesn't even bother to lift her eyes from the board. Once, her to-do list was filled with tasks associated with the funeral and ways to deal with my father's stuff—his 100 percent cashmere sweaters from a Changsha flea market that were definitely not 100 percent cashmere, his chunky Dell laptop, his exercise bike with a missing shoe strap in the basement. But these days it has shrunk to just two words: "Rice, Eggs."

"I want to make sweet rice wine," she declared on the night we had the Phil Collins soup.

"We don't have any rice left," I said. "And what's that?"

"Rice you ferment until it turns alcoholic. I haven't had it for years, and now I crave it."

"So it makes you drunk?" I was alarmed. I thought about how embarrassing my mother was sober and how much more embarrassing she must be drunk. I'd never seen her drink, not even on her birthday. I braced myself to protest this idea, to pick apart her plan.

"No, the alcohol content is pretty low."

"How do you make sure the alcohol content stays low?"

"The longer you let it sit, the stronger it becomes. The yeast will keep eating the sugar. If you leave it out for a few days, it won't be very strong. A month, then maybe pretty strong."

"And what if you leave it out for, like, years?" It was a moot question—we both knew we didn't have years. We might not even have a month.

"Then it'll knock you out." She narrowed her eyes. "You don't drink with your friends, do you?"

"Of course not." I spat out my lie like it was insulting that she would even think that.

"Do your friends drink?"

"No."

"You know alcohol hurts your brain. It lowers your IQ."

"I know. You've said that ten thousand times."

Before the red smudge appeared, I'd tried beer only once, from a lukewarm can Rick had fished out of his dad's broken mini fridge. The liquid fizzed in my stomach like carbonated juice. I found it uninteresting but pretended to like it. It has been harder to pretend with the clear stuff we salvage from the convenience store on Dana's block, whose windows were smashed the week the men in suits appeared on TV.

"Isn't it sad to think about the things we haven't done?" Dana said the last time we met up, before waves of noxious air started to appear at night. In the dark, she rolled a plastic mini bottle of Don Julio in her palm. We were sitting at the top of a slide on the playground in Goose Park. Rick was lying flat on his back on the asphalt beneath us, his hands behind his neck. It was nearing midnight. Every few minutes, I'd look in the direction of my house to make sure all the lights were still off, that my mother was still sound asleep and oblivious to my absence.

I knew what Dana meant. In school, some kids our age incessantly talked about drinking, having sex, and smoking. They were obsessed with breaking rules, a desire that eluded us. We had hardly learned how to follow the rules in the first place, and seemed to be forever a step behind normal:

Dana, with the Polish accent she couldn't shake off, and Rick and I, who were thought of as either cousins or secretly betrothed. All our parents avoided volunteering at school events. The drinking was Dana's idea, part of the long bucket list of "life experiences" she believed we had to check off in our limited time left.

I leave my mother in front of her dry-erase board, shut the door of my bedroom, and resolve to mow the lawn tomorrow. When we first moved into this house from that palm-sized city apartment above a pho shop, not long after my ninth birthday, my father spent an entire weekend studying the rules of suburban homeownership. He had been raised in a village in Changsha where the bedroom he and his two brothers shared doubled as a chicken coop in the winter; my mother, who grew up in Beijing, had shared a hallway bathroom with three other families. Which is to say, they were not well acquainted with space. That first weekend, he brought home a thick book with a dark blue cover titled *City Code Enforcement* and announced that there were simply *things that must be done*: mow the lawn at the same frequency as your neighbors, repaint your house trim in one of six colors, separate your trash from your recycling, shovel the snow on the sidewalks promptly so people don't slip in front of your house and sue you.

"Guan ta de," my mother replied. Translation: "Let them." Translation: "Who cares?" Translation: "I don't care." Over our spread of dishes, my father and I frowned at her like parents at a disobedient child.

When I turn on the lawn mower the following morning, it moans from indigestion. The grass has gotten so tall that its willowy stalks bow over the machine like a small green yurt. I am checking the engine when a delivery truck stops in front of our driveway. A man dressed in all brown drops off what looks like four hefty boxes on our front porch. I'm about to sprint to the boxes, fling open our door, and shout the good news to my mother, when I notice a flutter of movement in the corner of my eye.

"Hey!"

The woman next door, with her twin braids and her long red-checkered skirt billowing in the breeze, stands on her porch with both hands on her hips. I can hear her Chihuahua barking through the screen door that she has half propped open with her elbow.

"Is that a food delivery?" she asks. Cutting across the thick curtain of humid air is the high-pitched simmer of her envy.

"I think so." I try to keep my voice neutral. I cannot remember the last time she spoke to me aside from a terse "Good morning" whenever I saw her walking the dog as I left for school.

The front door behind me swings open. Without a word, my mother bends over the boxes like a giant comma, shielding them with her body. She pinches my thigh, gesturing at me to help her. "Ow!" I say.

It is not until we are inside, the boxes piled in our foyer, that she says in a hushed voice, as if the neighbor can still hear us: "Don't tell the Lees about the food."

"Why not?"

"What if they rob us? What if they hurt us because they're jealous?" She taps her left temple with her index finger. "Don't be so simple."

"I doubt—"

"When it comes to a time like this, people will do things you can't even imagine. You know a boy in your uncle's village got shot during the Great Famine for stealing a single sweet potato from a neighbor?"

I let out an impatient huff of air. Though she has a point—with the recent increase in violent crimes, robberies, raids, and whatnot—she is not exactly unbiased toward the Lees. When we first moved here, she was overjoyed to see the last name LEE inscribed in curlicues on the neighbor's pristine white mailbox. "I think our neighbors are Chinese!" she announced, her voice echoing in our empty living room.

"They could be Taiwanese," my father said. "Or Korean."

She shrugged. "It'll be good to have an Asian family near us, anyway." In the city, she had taken comfort in the presence of the Vietnamese family who lived above us, the Thai grocery store down the street, the occasional stooped Chinese grandma clutching a bag of fruit on the bus.

Later that day, when she spotted a family of blonds going out for a drive, she was indignant. "But Lee is a Chinese last name!"

"Not necessarily. There's Robert E. Lee." At age nine, I was already eager to use my superior knowledge of American culture to undermine her authority.

She glared at me. "Who's that?"

"A famous American," I said confidently, though that was all I knew about him.

Since then, she eyed the not-Chinese Lees with suspicion. But the suspicion seemed mutual— the Lees never introduced themselves to us, even though I once witnessed them bringing a pie to a young family who had moved into a vacant house down the street. We still don't know one another's first names.

In the kitchen we unpack the boxes to discover a bounty: several dozen eggs, a whole bag of white rice, frozen broccoli, frozen peas, microwavable bacon, green onions, sticky rice, sugar, carrots, six cans of whole peeled tomatoes, and cereal. With the stores closed, delivery is the only way to get sustenance, a fact my mother resents. When we first moved into this house, she saw the Lees' garden next door—all white-fenced with creeping green vines, like something out of a *Better Homes and Gardens* magazine spread—and asked my father for a vegetable patch. He refused. The idea that he would have to tend to the land again after clawing his way out of the rice paddies, crossing an entire ocean, and buying a three-bedroom house in an American suburb was shameful, bordering on heresy.

"See, this is what happens when you try to save face. Your family dies," my mother griped when our food supply was running low last month, and the Lees were harvesting baskets of blackberries and nectarines in their backyard. Now, as we carefully cut our unexpected bounty from its layers of plastic packaging with scissors, neither of us says what we are probably both fearing: this may be our last shipment.

We have a lunch of carefully rationed rice and broccoli, mixed with a couple of drops of soy sauce. Her chopsticks in midair, my mother says, "I was worried. Before we got the food, I thought I needed to figure out how my aunt lived on tree bark during the Great Famine."

I look out the kitchen window to our patio and the surrounding maple trees, their trunks fervently brown. The corn in neighboring fields wilted overnight last month, the fish in the nearby river have disappeared, but the trees, at least, seem healthy. I imagine peeling back their bark, revealing the sappy white flesh underneath, catching their lifeblood on my tongue. "The more bitter the medicine, the better," my mother used to say, lifting trembling spoonfuls of brown herbal medicine to my lips whenever I had a cold, or steaming bowls of ginseng shaped like dead worms if my cheeks lost their color. Once, in middle school, I opened my lunchbox to one of these worms, and the girl sitting next to me screamed. When I confronted my mother, my father offered to pick up some peanut butter at the grocery store. "And jelly," I added sharply. "You eat the peanut butter and jelly together."

All afternoon, my mother prepares to make her sweet rice wine with our new bounty—poking her hand into cabinets, running her fingers along dusty shelves, lifting couch cushions. "Where's my jiu qu," she keeps saying, rifling through our pantry.

"Where's my jiu qu?" I hear her murmuring, the drawers opening and closing, opening and closing, until I can't stand it anymore. I yell, "What do you need? Can't we just order it online?"

It takes ten minutes of her watching the computer screen over my shoulder, trying to translate into English the term for the ingredient she is missing, and of me inputting various combinations of keywords like "small white yeast balls" and "yeast agent" into a popular search engine before we finally find what we're looking for. I click through dozens of online catalogs selling various types of koji, all indicating they're sold out. She throws up her hands and goes back to her rifling.

On a cooking blog, I read about the history of koji— also known as *Aspergillus oryzae*—which is apparently expansive. The fungus was first written about in 300 BCE, in China. The earliest evidence of fermented soybeans made using *Aspergillus oryzae* was discovered in Changsha (coincidentally, where my father grew up), in a noblewoman's tomb that dated back to 165 BCE. The first European document to mention the word *koji* was a book written by Jesuit missionaries in Japan in the 1600s. I scroll to the latest entry in the timeline. Just two years ago, a couple from New York City had written a cookbook titled *Worldly Kitchen* and called koji "a secret weapon that no one seems to be talking about, that will give any of your meals a thrilling, homemade twist." I find a one-page preview of the book that I am able to access online without paying. "Look for the growth of mycelium on the food after a few days," the couple advises. "It should resemble the fallen fur of a small white dog."

I hear a sudden shriek from the basement. I run down and see my mother squatting between large vats of canola oil and soy sauce containers, holding up a small plastic bag containing white lollipop-sized balls. "I knew he put them somewhere," she says triumphantly.

In the kitchen, I watch her pour the entire bag of sticky rice into a metal bowl and fill it with water. She sets it on our dining table beneath a picture of my dead father, like an offering. Last winter, his mitral valve collapsed like a pricked balloon while he was two blocks from home, the blue Toyota Corolla plowing through a neighbor's fence and not stopping until it plunged into the empty concrete pool in their backyard. After the funeral, during which my mother laid out platters of peanut-butter-and-jelly sandwiches cut into triangles, we went for days without speaking. Things about our life that had once been invisible rose before me like treacherous hills and made me stew in silence. Who will pick up the right packets of cheese and bread from the grocery store? Who will make the turkey for Thanksgiving and watch the same online tutorials on how to carve it, year after year? Who will I invite to my parent-teacher conferences? Who will mow the lawn and shovel the sidewalk and remind us of all the things we have to do?

It wasn't my mother's incompetence at doing these things that angered me so much as her disregard for what to me were basic principles of dignity. She started to do tai chi in our driveway in front of passing traffic each morning. In grocery stores, she snapped at me loudly in Mandarin between rows of cereal, turning heads. She frowned at people's dogs. Though she had been this way before my father's death, she became more unrestrained. I expressed my disapproval by heating up frozen pizzas for dinner and busying myself with the things my father used to do: separating the trash from the recycling, returning library books, smiling at dog walkers. But when the red disk appeared in the sky, when we were told to stay indoors, when creatures we had never noticed before made their absence clear—cicadas, sparrows, frogs, beings whose disappearance made the outside world feel like an empty glass bowl that would shatter with the tap of a fingernail—my mother and I holed up in the house like everyone else and watched as the distance between our orbits shrank.

So I am with her now, in the kitchen, instead of marinating in a pool of internet news in my room or video-calling Rick and Dana. Here at the sink, we rinse the rice, drain, rinse again, drain, over and over, until the water runs clear.

At night we watch the TV screen flicker dramatically as broadcasters detail disasters: disturbances in the moon's gravitational pull are molding tidal waves into mile-long walls that occasionally collapse, washing away coastal cities; earthworms are dying at record rates; in the faraway Chinese city where my father's brothers live, the leaves have turned a brilliant purple, and the pigs have vanished. The screen casts a blue glow on our arms as we stir the rice patiently to feel for its firmness, as if we are rubbing the back of someone who's coughing.

"The year I was in Yunnan, I don't know if I've ever told you about it..." She drifts off, as if expecting me to interrupt. But I stay quiet, run a wet finger through the engorged rice pearls and feel their clinging.

While a reporter on TV interviews people digging holes in their yards, she describes a military base camp and washing her face with freezing water from a shared metal basin. Her Mandarin vocabulary bulges, oozing out of the tiny realm of basic words about our everyday suburban life with which I am familiar. I am able to catch only the gist of what she says: something about the year the party got pissed off at college students, something about copying quotes from political textbooks in chalk until fingers turned bone white, something about lengthy discussions on the distinction between Marxism and Socialism. She tells me the students wrote wills every time they went to help with a satellite launch, in case something went wrong, though somehow nothing ever went wrong. Still, they kept doing it because it made them feel heroic.

"Not soft enough yet," she says, letting a fistful of rice rain back into the bowl. "The grains need to fall apart between your fingers when you pinch. See?"

After my mother places the bowl back under my father's picture, I search "Yunnan" on the internet. I click through images of Shangri-La City and Tiger Leaping Gorge under "top sights to see in Yunnan, China." I have seen the term *Shangri-La* plastered over a restaurant awning and always assumed it was an invented name, like *General Tsao's chicken*. In the images, Buddhist temples with golden roofs rise from mountaintops like fingers stretching from the earth to touch the sky.

Before her job at the elder center, my mother worked as a substitute math teacher. At school, she was little more than a talking mannequin—I know because that's how my friends and I treated substitute teachers when they showed up in our classrooms like lost, overgrown children. She often brought home stories of her students making fun of her English, and if the story was about a grammatical error, she and my father would argue until they inevitably turned to me as a judge. If my mother won, she would hide how pleased she was by lifting her bowl so it obscured half her face. Her fingers were sturdy, her nails clipped as short as day-old crescent moons. Now I picture her operating a satellite station at nineteen, a first-year electrical engineering student, running those fingers over a switchboard like a pianist.

I am awoken the next morning by the distant roar of lawn mowers. I run downstairs without putting on pants and look out our living room window. The grass has gotten so tall that I can see only the roof of the house across the road.

"The grass," I say to my mother. She is watering a pot of green onions on our windowsill which have been propagating so abundantly that we can soon make entire salads out of them. She looks outside and considers our lawn as if it were a painting of a lawn in a museum that has nothing to do with her.

"It's taller. Good."

"Good!"

"Don't waste your time trying to mow it. You won't be able to."

When I go outside to take a closer look, I see that she is right: the grass is now a few inches taller than me, each blade as thick as my wrist. They must be hollow on the inside, because when a breeze picks up, the blades bump into one another with the tinkling sound of wind chimes. The red disk is a blooming wound in the gray sky.

Back at the house, my mother smooths out globs of soaked rice—each grain now softened and fat—like a rug over cheesecloth. I pick up objects in my bedroom and restore them to their original positions: three dirty T-shirts, six used water glasses, fifteen too-fat folders vomiting essays and graph paper with my calculus homework, which I haven't touched in months. By now most of our teachers are gone; one by one, in mass emails to the students, they explained that they planned to live out their last days in Costa Rica or Hawaii.

But during the brief period after the red smudge first appeared and before the teachers vanished,

I found a rare burst of diligence with my school-work. In the mornings, over breakfast noodles steaming in thin brown broth, I carefully traced out asymptotic functions that approach each other infinitely but never touch. There was comfort in learning that infinity, at least mathematically, could still exist. On the TV humming in the background, the countdown to the end had already begun.

"What do you think?" My mother guides my fingers across the rice rug, laid out on our dining table. I press on it for soft spots, as if I were check-ing an avocado for firmness.

"It can't be cold, but it can't be too hot," she explains. "Too hot, and jiu qu will die."

"The yeast is... alive?" My mother has chopped the koji balls into a small hill of sawdust on our cutting board. I think of them wedged in a corner in our basement for years. It seems impossible that something that's that dead can be alive, can *digest* things. I imagine our world ending in a bright red flash, like all the men in suits have described, and the yeast still in a metal bowl somewhere in this house, surviving, digesting and digesting and breaking chemicals down and making sugars and doing what it needs to do to stay alive. Was that how the world began?

My mother lays the back of her hand on the rice, as if feeling a forehead for fever. "Good," she says. Then she sprinkles the chopped-up koji all over the rice—a pack of wolves being let loose among sheep.

Over the next few days, the grass gradually filters out the sunlight from the first floor of our house like a curtain creeping up from the soil. At the slight-est breeze, the stalks' shadows waver on our walls. The house feels alive, breathing. When I check our mailbox, the Lees' two little girls watch me from their driveway, fists in their mouths. Their mother throws a frightened look toward our lawn, as if its unchecked growth could spread and swallow her children.

Against my mother's warning that the wine needs to sit longer, I squat by the furnace where she placed the bowl, unwrap its four layers of blankets, and lift the lid just a crack. I want to see for myself the mycelium devouring the rice, spreading all over it like "the fallen fur of a small white dog." The bowl explodes with a sweet-sour smell. When I hold a flashlight above it, I see that the mycelium looks less like fur and more like a fine dusting of snow.

"Not ready yet," my mother says when I inform her. "But soon."

To pass the time, we clean the house. Together we carry the turtle tank from the living room to the basement closet. I try to avoid thinking about how pieces of Phil Collins recently floated to the top of our soup bowl by conjuring his earlier, happier days. Once, he swam in the tank, his shell a coaster-sized thing, and my father stood over him and offered up a name: "How about Phil Collins?" My father always claimed that Phil Collins was his favorite American singer, never mind that Phil Collins is actually British, and I'd never once heard my father listening to his music.

I organize the newspapers that we used to toss onto the couch before they stopped arriving altogether. As my mother dusts the bookshelf of DVDs, the TV shows footage of whales, their mouths opening and closing, on a deserted beach. She clicks it off with the remote control and mutters, "Mei yong de dong xi." Translation: "Useless thing." Translation: "This is your father's way of wasting money." Translation: "What's the point of wallowing?"

Before we knew the world was ending, my mother and I rarely watched TV. My father was the one who insisted on getting cable television. He developed a penchant for American sitcoms that were popular during his youth, when he was still a teenager in that Changsha village and knew about America only in the abstract. After he purchased the TV, I would come downstairs to get a glass of water before bed and see his face bathed in its blue light, him chuckling a beat behind the laugh track.

I ask my mother about a girl she mentioned in her recent tale of that harrowing year in the Yunnan military base camp. Apparently, a few of her female classmates slept with local soldiers to avoid hard labor. While the others baked under the hot sun, marching until their legs felt like steel rods jutting into their hips, hauling sacks of rice atop their shoulders until they buckled to the ground, these girls rode to the nearest town on the backs of military jeeps and were bought squares of red bean cake. Eventually, one got pregnant.

My mother seems surprised that I remember this insignificant detail. "Well, one day the government decided it was done punishing us, so we left."

"She left too?"

"Of course. She got rid of the baby and came home like everyone else. Everyone thought she was ruined, but she married a man she met on the first train out of Yunnan, finished school, and moved to America."

I stop rustling the newspapers in my hands. My mother has never mentioned a classmate who also came to America. I ask if they keep in touch. "No. I heard she's doing well, but I never wondered much about her." I search my mother's face for signs of envy or resentment, but it is placid, lake-like.

Moral of the story: you're not punished for simply trying to survive. This is what I think later, as I wheel the blue and black bins to the end of our driveway. It is the tail end of twilight. Along the street, the windows in our neighborhood light up one by one in their quiet, fearful way, and I can almost see the tables set with matching silverware, the salads in big wooden bowls, the embers in the fireplaces, the board games, the sitcoms playing on TV, the polite refrains of "Can you pass the napkins?," the families holding their hands in prayer—all that I once thought I was approaching. Meanwhile, the red thing is as red as the throbbing behind my eyes when I close them against the dimming sun.

This is what I remember before the lights cut out: An autumn in my early childhood when we were still living in the city, ignorant of the future and its strange rules. We were crouching in a park with brittle brown leaves strewn all around us as my father dropped an acorn a foot from the ground, showing me how gravity worked. He handed the acorn to me and told me to try, but instead I sank my teeth into its grooves. My mother, who watched from a park bench, said, "Aiya, don't let it ruin her milk teeth." I laughed because I saw them laughing together.

"Is it ready?" I ask my mother. Along the coast of the Yucatán Peninsula, penguins are showing up floating like ducks, and a power outage is spreading across the continent in what I imagine must look like a massive ink spillage from space. Next door, the Lees' lawn has been torn up overnight, not a speck of green remaining on the scrambled, uneven hills of soil. I know the wine can go on fermenting for more days, for a long while, maybe even forever, but I have a feeling we are running out of time.

My mother lights all the leftover birthday candles we've been saving in our kitchen drawer, and we crack eggs into the rice, stir it until the whites and yolks become silver and gold threads. We serve the sweet rice wine flushed with egg in our best bowls. With the kitchen windows open, I can feel the air running its charged fingers across the backs of my arms. The grass jungle is still and silent, the giant stalks bowing over us like sentries. The sky is red, but we are safe, I think, under our canopy.

The wine is sweet and goes down easily, nothing like the clear liquor that once burned my throat. As we wait for the world to end, my mother brings up Yunnan again, this time without pausing for my interruption or prompting—because we both know I can never truly understand; because it will take an infinity to even approach understanding, or whatever of infinity there is left; because I can still try. There were mountains there that colored lakes emerald with their reflections, cranes with wing-spans as long as grown men, the thinning oxygen up on the peaks that made your head ring with clarity. There were students who looked forward to the third Wednesday of every month, when they'd go into town to get soap bars wrapped in heavy waxed paper. There was the end, when it was all over and she bought a bowl of sweet rice wine flushed with egg on the train ride home. The person who was sitting next to her would become her husband, the owner of the exercise bike sitting in our basement, but she did not know that yet. She savored every drop of the sweet liquid off the single metal spoon she had brought with her all the way to Yunnan and watched the vast, ancient green plains rolling past as the train back to Beijing carried her to the rest of her life.

18 OR 34 MILES FROM PERENNIAL SQUARE

by MAX DELSOHN

ASHER POKED FIRE WITH damp stick. Big log fell over, crushed little flame underneath. Yeah, he thought, snuffing stuff out = basically that easy.

Trees canopied, cut through late afternoon + kept camp area darker. Asher sat in black folding chair too big for body. Nervous, looking out to rest of forest. Ace fussed around in tent-thing. Clinking of flatware. Muffled happy shout *these guys thought of everything!*

Ace = backpacking fiend but Asher tries to avoid (*ticks, Trump flags, no THANK you*) so they had compromised with Rent-a-Camp a.k.a. glamping a.k.a. tent-thing. Hosts of Rent-a-Camp usually nearby but this week out of town, so metric fuck-ton of private acres all for them. Tent-thing made of canvas and gray net with fat spiders in corner, mice skittering over roof + visible through canvas ceiling. Ace said *yurt-esque*. Asher said *what the fuck is a yurt*.

Ace came out of tent-thing with tongs and marshmallow bag.

No pokers, but this should work, said Ace. He handed Asher tongs, then turned to resuscitate fire. Mosquito landed on fine white hair of Ace Neck.

Asher stared at mosquito, relaxed kinda, said nothing. Who could blame gross little bug for wanting Ace Blood inside? Who wouldn't pick Ace Neck to kiss? Asher had covered himself in DEET, but Ace just did arms/legs. *Be judicious with that stuff, it's poison*, said Ace.

Ace turned around and smiled at Asher watching. Asher cast marshmallowed tongs into now renewed blaze.

Ace and Asher had been together for 4 months and what was that supposed to mean? Not so long that you *had* to love but long enough where love might come up. 4 months on the Gaygorian Calendar might mean love, might mean move in, might mean engagement and animal shelter trips. Big words, big questions, big ideas, big practical applications. Might mean sex. Might mean sex constantly. Okay yes sex constantly can confirm. Both dudes = new to fucking dudes after long string of mean cis GFs and wasn't it fun that they could be real trans, real masc together? Now Asher knew he was dude-gay for life. Like Asher = politically NO on institutional marriage but privately what if (*oh fuck*) he was starting to get the forever part?

He'd even considered beginning to hint at slight possibility of such forever when Ace announced he wanted phalloplasty and would start raising money for it on GoFundMe.

Not unlike Asher was doing, actually.

At first Asher = super turned-on by twin-phallo idea (*sword fight shit, 1-hand-2-dick jerk-offs, overall cooler threesomes, HELLO*), was already planning recovery logistics (*you get yours next summer, I get mine next winter, we assemble care team for overlap in downtime, meal trains, your sister can visit, OH YEAH*), just 1 major snafu on horizon: Asher phalloplasty funds weren't raising. His GoFundMe'd been up for 6 months and he was still like 8K away from goal, which he got was big community ask, but Ace? 2 weeks and boom. Big money. Phalloplasty paid.

Asher assumed this success was due to Ace being (1) blond, (2) good at internet, (3) good smiler, (4) squarer jawed, (5) not balding, (6) not a fuzzy little Jew with yacht-sized hips, and (7) not wanting phalloplasty with moldy desperation of 20-year secret kid-hood longing.

Asher tried to act normal but Ace caught on. *Jealousy is ugly, Ashy. I can't believe you're taking my success so personally.*

So past week = garbage fights about nothing. Past week = absolutely no fucking. 7 days and *0 fuck counts*. Unprecedented in relationship. Could mean trouble. Could mean whole dudely dude-fucking happily ever after thing = completely out window.

And past week = only 1 GoFundMe donation for Asher. $10 from mean cis ex-GF's mom.

Loud thud somewhere in forest. Asher flinched. Snapped out of doom spiral or went deeper down, like who knows. Fuckin' spooky nature shit.

Whatcha thinking about? asked Ace. Slight eyebrow-raise of concern. Asher marshmallow super on fire, papery black + bulbous white all exploding like monster zombie silkworm.

How far are we from Perennial Square?

Honey, I already told you. We're close but not that close. Do you want a hot dog with your marshmallow?

Not hungry.

Ashy.

Perennial Square was, Asher thought, about 34 miles from tent-thing. Either that or it was 18 miles. He'd looked it up once + forgot. Now No Service out here to check. Also wasn't expert with numbers. What he was expert at = keeping track of fascists. Like where they held meetings/rallies, occupied small government buildings, got beers after macing random Seattle passersby in face.

Last meeting of Precious Boys, in Perennial Square. Went to bar there, then came to city next day to harass *transgendered Talibans*. They'd pulled knife on Mikey at intersection of Madison + 17th, right in front of co-op.

Mikey was okay because Mikey ran inside.

Then Precious Boys went back to Perennial Square, 18 or 34 miles from here.

Here = the goddamn woods. The goddamn woods = nowhere to hide.

Ace didn't get it, had never squared off against fascists of any kind, honestly Ace's politics weren't amazing, he wanted to get into homesteading, liked to donate food occasionally but wouldn't laugh at viral video of guy punching Nazi in face (*LEGENDARY*) or when that other guy threw hot coffee on Alex Jones on 3rd Ave. (*LEGENDARY + LOCAL!*).

I don't think violence is ever justified, had said Ace.

Violence is justified against people who want to kill you, Asher said back.

Now Ace was saying *you're clearly not listening to me. I'll be in the tent when you're ready to start.* Now Ace was stomping off.

Enjoy tent-thing, Ace.

Asher could hardly blame little-lamb Ace, in fact was *glad* Ace didn't have the who what when where whys of local fascists down pat the way he did. It had all started, like so many awful things do, with a big bang.

6 months prior Asher had been in center of dense mob of lefties going toe-to-toe with cops who had their backs to Precious Boy rally at Westlake Center, right in downtown middle a.k.a. right in shit-middle of shit. Asher heard Ralphie's voice, trusted organizer, smartest they to follow in shit-middle, say *white bodies to the front, white bodies to the front*, so Asher to-the-fronted. Ralphie had vision, dense mob had numbers, Precious Boys had fear. Asher'd done this before: lock arms on front line, keep chanting, don't move. Wear. Them. Out.

Then, 6 feet from front line, BANG! BANG BANG!

For .0000001 second, Asher like, what? Then Asher ran, like, *ran*. Precious Boys *ran*. Whole fuckin' crowd = *ran*. Cops flash-banging, cops walk-running, quarterback-type arms launching. Ralphie yelling *move, move*. Asher heard pitter-patter fast of own sneakers on street, sprinting down Pine, then alley. But sneaker sounds = it. Otherwise freak-quiet. Just bang after bang after bang and scamper/drumroll of feet.

Some seconds later, new sounds, new *feet*. Asher turned around like, Ralphie? Instead, Precious Boy, bearded and silly-shirted. Sprinting. Was gaining. Mouth open like screaming but Asher couldn't hear it. Eyes gleeful like child. Hunting.

Asher ran faster. Precious Boy chased him onto 1st Ave. but lost him in mess of Pike Place. Asher crouched behind favorite fruit stand till for sure safe.

Asher? Ace called from tent-thing. *Did you bring bullets to our Rent-a-Camp?*

Hmmmm. Fuck.

Asher got out of too-big chair and walked into tent-thing.

Inside was king-size bed with 2 Ace sleeping bags, 2 Ace pillows, 2 Ace wool blankets. On bedside table, Ace Fenty sleep mask. On floor, kindling, battery-powered lanterns, fire extinguisher, crate of flatware. In corner, spiders, wood-burning stove. On table, Asher backpack. Ace standing next to backpack. Ace holding small paper box of bullets with horrified look on face.

You have a fucking gun?

Asher did have "fucking gun," in fact had been wearing holster this entire time, which Ace would have known if he'd bothered to touch him since driving to Rent-a-Camp. Duh! On 4-hour drive they passed *directly* through Herald Park, *infamous birthplace of Precious Boy cofounder Patrick Tooley*, no way was he traveling as passenger in Ace's *neon blue Subaru, of all things*, unarmed.

Asher didn't tell people about gun because most queers = weird about guns.

Ace included, apparently.

When were you going to tell me? Ace went on. *Before or after we moved in together? Before or after we got a cat?*

You want to move in together? Asher asked. Ace had never said it outright before. Just cat talk before! Just cat!

I don't know now! This sucks, Ash. Ace paced in tent-thing, knocked over battery-powered lantern then immediately picked up.

It's for self-defense only. Promise. And for Ace defense!
I don't need you to protect me. Not with this.
Ace stared for long time. Steel-blank. Then:

Show me the gun.

Show it to me.

Show me the fucking gun, Asher!

Asher showed Ace fucking gun.

Pulled out 9 mm handgun, Springfield Armory's XD-M Elite 3.8" with 2 (*2, Ace!*) safeties (*for maximum safety!*) in leather holster obscured by Asher's oversize *Steven Universe* T-shirt (*for maximum obscurity!*). He had never fired gun but had practiced with similar model at Shoreline range several times + 1x/week sat on floor of bedroom and held it unloaded adjusting position of hands until folded just right for dry fire.

He had purchased gun the day after flash-bangs and gleeful-eyed Precious Boy with scream full of nothing.

Holy shit, is this loaded?!

And now they were 18 or 34 miles from Perennial Square.

Get out. I can't be around you right now, Ace said. Ouch. Asher strode toward zipped-up flap of tent-thing, unzipped, walked out, kept walking.

* * *

Asher walked for hour at least. Still light out but not for long. Ace didn't follow. Phone still No Service but some battery left in case flashlight relevant. Covered trash can outside tent-thing suggested no concern for grizzlies in area but he'd be fine. Was maybe lost but Asher = fine, tough even. Had "fucking gun" after all.

Asher = good shot. Had knocked the hearts out of plenty paper men at range. Yeah, moving target different but adrenaline could make miracles. On flash-bang day had never run so fast in life.

Pine needles acorns maple leaves snail shells mud dirt whatever else crunched up under feet. Birds swooping, chirping, *toooweeet!* Brighter here, greener here, plenty of sound here. Maybe Ace had a point about all this nature stuff.

Blugh. Ace.

Then Asher heard yell. High-pitched man yell. Sounds of the forest emptied out. Could only hear the sound of own life + listening for sound of next attack.

Then, swear to god: a dick. What? Bounded over on its balls, like feet. Took reprieve on small stump with moss fizzing off sides. Dick erect, its head like a *head*, eyeless, but looking at him somehow. Sizing him up.

Sound came back. Distant clomping through trees. Dick flinched. More yelling.

C'mere, boy!

Dick scurried between Asher legs, hooked a left, booked it alongside thin creek.

Asher pulled at own hair. Wild dick! Dick in wild! Dick using balls to run! Dick repurposing balls as feet!

Ace had said something about creeks on ride over—*if you're ever lost in a forest, track the animals. They'll eventually lead you to water.*

Could dick be heading toward water?

Could dick drink?

Yelling + clomping getting louder.

Asher sprinted.

Asher followed creek. Feet pounded, bulldozed through ferns + mini stick-trees. Thank god wearing jeans. Tick-proof. Scrape-proof. Not bulletproof. But he had gun. Asher. He. Behind him?

Don't look. Never look. Get to water. Get dick. Run run run run run.

He was faster than whatever yelling. Yelling smaller and smaller, then gone.

A glittering blue appeared through gap in trees. Asher slowed to walk/jog. Pond with clear water, dirt bottom, black stones. Noodly inch-fish, water-striders, mosquitoes, white gnat clouds, flies, black leggy critters. And there, on other side of water, was dick.

Asher crouched down.

Dick = erect, manic, frenzied, shoving its head repeatedly + violently into pond, thrusting so fast it was getting like inch of air between balls and ground per thrust. He guessed this was dick, er, drinking? It looked like it was fucking the water.

Dick was good-sized dick. Small. He had told Ace he didn't want anything too big re: phallo, he didn't want too much change, had even considered simple meta, would have done it if chances for successful penetration weren't quite so slim, he knew some guys pulled meta penetration off but if you're gonna get surgery + know what you want why take risk?

Size-wise, Ace hadn't agreed. Ace wanted some-thing big. Impossible to ignore/forget/disappoint/ self-hate.

Good thing Ace had all the money he needed, then.

Would this dick qualify as *feral* dick? There were jokes about such on Reddit, deep in r/FTM where new gender-questioners + concerned cis part-ners would never think to click. Some guy said he'd seen one before, had been laughed off forum. Feral dicks less likely than Bigfoot. Very funny, troll.

Now Asher was like, fuck, Bigfoot = real?

If he caught dick, might there be some kind of transplant situation? He'd never talked to anybody, in person or in forum, who'd done transplant. Read something once about taking immunosuppressant meds for rest of life? But he'd barely talked to anyone who'd had phallo! Most of his friends in Seattle just got top surgery + hysto then called it day.

But Asher wanted dick. A peeing cumming *pen-etrating* dick. Recovery from phallo took time. Took money. And here was dick. Right here.

He remembered gun in holster. Brought right hand to it slow, all cool, cowboy-like. Dick had stopped fucking water, had hopped a few feet back toward forest and was now napping, flaccid, in shade.

Little fucker was small. But balls = weirdly big. Buff from running? Asher didn't want balls with phallo, thought ball part sort of odd, no sensation or anything, just sacks of silicone. Plus he planned to keep his V, he got taste for bottoming that way on occasion, plus he knew Ace post-phallo = especially pleased.

Ideally Asher'd just stick dick onto already-there junk. Nothing fancy.

He imagined live, feral dick was better than dead one. He could just *fell* dick. Not in killing sense! 1 clean, straight shot to balls so it couldn't motor off. Then Asher'd descend, carry it in his hands back to camp, show Ace everything was gonna be okay, emotionally/financially, they could start having dudely dude sex again, move dudely in together, et cetera.

As he pulled gun out of holster, he was already writing pitch in his head.

If feral dicks are a thing, then who's to say some open-minded doctor can't stitch it on real quick? Who's to say I'm not in for another miracle?

Asher folded his hands around gun. Arms straight. Trigger finger measured, even, slow. Just like at range.

Hey! called a voice. Dick perked up. Asher stood up/turned with gun.

From his right approached plucky young transsexual with butterfly net.

Oh, shit. Ha ha, where's the fire? plucky young transsexual said. Raised his hands in air. Oh. Asher = aiming gun at guy holding butterfly net. He quick put weapon away.

Sorry. Thought you were someone else.

Should've known I'd find a fellow brother out here, said Plucky. *But I call dibs on this bad boy. Been tracking this peen for weeks! Gonna fasten this shit to my shit or die trying! Saw him at an oyster fest out in Shelton if you can believe that. Scrambled under the tables so fast, folks thought he was a rat. But I knew right away.* He aimed butterfly net at dick, settled into nap in shade. Pretended to fire net like rifle.

You live around here?

Sort of. Not really. Perennial Square. Bout 30-ish miles from here.

18 or 34! 34!

Lot of Precious Boy activity out there? Asher said, trying to sound casual, his eyes on dick. Palms sweating.

Nah, it's a big little town. They're only ever at one bar. Not big shit-where-you-eat-ers. More of a problem for the likes of you, city boy. He turned butterfly net on Asher, fake-fired.

If you get them 1-on-1, they're not even that bad.

Asher winced. He turned to face Plucky.

Listen, man. I need this dick. Let me have this one. You live here, you'll get another chance.

Another chance? Fat chance! Plucky said with good-natured laugh. *You know how rare these are? He's the first dick I've seen in the flesh, and I had to trespass on this fine private property to get it. I'm sorry to say, but first come, first serve. Snooze you lose, fuzzball.*

Asher snatched gun from holster. Pushed it toward Plucky Head. Plucky put his hands back up. New look on face.

Hey, Plucky said through gritted teeth. Eyes darting. *You don't want to do this, buddy. Throw your life away for some dick that science hasn't even figured out how to attach to you yet? Transplant is a Hail Mary, we both know that.*

Asher hesitated. If Plucky lunged, he would shoot. Self-defense. Reason for season.

Guys like us gotta stick together. That's the important thing. Just walk back to where you came from and we can forget this ever happened. I don't even know your name. Fellow brother, that's all you are to me. Please, guy. Please. Please!

Plucky Brow sweating. Plucky Knees shaking. Blugh.

Asher lowered gun.

Woof! Plucky said with dramatic exhale. *I almost peed, brother! Jesus hell. Knew you weren't the shooting type. Talk about Precious Boy domain!*

Asher nodded.

Now, why don't you let this country kid show you how real dick hunting is done.

Asher watched as Plucky crouched low, retreated into trees, then circled around pond so he could surprise dick from behind. Asher already had shame-headache. Head felt like concrete/cotton ball/useless waste of space.

Asher wondered briefly if any feral vaginas were running around in forest, or at least feral clitorises.

He wondered if he could cut off own V somehow,

set V loose or gift to friend. If he didn't get dick, Ace = break up with jealous/ugly Asher anyway, no need for that second hole. No need for animal shelter trip.

He wondered if his whole life would be like this, getting scared and dumped and chased and swindled and gaslit. Guarding small sad nest of own life from mean eagle grasp of world.

Plucky was directly behind dick. 10–12 feet-ish. Smiling, tongue out kinda. Both hands on net.

Guarding small sad Asher nest, then dying. Dying whenever. Dying in forest or alley in Pike Place. Alone in small sad nest with nothing but gross yolky soft body + not dudely at all.

Plucky 6 feet from dick now. Eyes gleeful. Going after what he wants.

Good for Plucky.

Asher straightened arms + fired, fired again.

Darker, darker, darker every step! Asher tried to retrace path with phone flashlight. His hairy stomach poked out where he'd torn shirt to bandage dick's wound. Hadn't tried to remove bullet, felt like he'd seen movies where removing actually worse blood loss—wise (or was that knife?), so decided to keep bullet in until consultation with Ace.

After brief celebration kiss, obv.

More blood than expected. Asher's hands still candy red. Somehow under fingernails. Kind of tough look, actually. Asher = stride back into camp with blood + gun + dick + ultra-masc forever love for Acey? Nonviolent Ace = completely out window. Asher dudely hotness = total override.

Dick was whining. Very flaccid. Asher stroked it, not in jerk-off way but, er, comforting? He hoped that was coming across, didn't want dick to get wrong idea so early in relationship. Or was it wrong idea? Ethics of hand-fucking your own, unattached feral dick = still unclear.

He whispered to dick, like motherly *you're gonna be okay, little guy. We'll be home soon with Acey. It's gonna be okay.*

Incoherent Plucky screaming in distance. Dick whined louder.

I'm gonna keep you safe.

A FABLE

by JOHN LEE CLARK

There was a certain king in this very Savatthi. And that king addressed a man: "Come now, my good man, bring together all those persons in Savatthi who have been blind from birth."

"Yes, your majesty," that man replied, and after detaining all the blind people in Savatthi, he approached the king and said, "All the blind people in Savatthi have been brought together, your majesty."

"Now, my man, show the blind people an elephant."

—"The Blind Men and the Elephant," *Tittha Sutta*
(translated from the Pali by John D. Ireland)

THE SUN'S WARM BREATH found the six men in their usual places, playing their elaborate game of shifting and scooping up stones. Their hands slid over and under one another as stone clicked against stone. They spoke fast, in a rustling stream no sighted ear could catch.

Ridhan was the first to scent it. "We've got a visitor."

The five others paused to listen. Parth, the oldest among their company, said, "Who?"

"Don't you smell it? It's an elephant, I'm sure."

They sniffed the air. "How do you know it's an elephant?" Nehal prodded Ridhan in his side. "You've never seen one."

"I don't know how I know." Ridhan jumped up. "Let's go see."

"Wait," Parth said. "There's money in this."

Ridhan groaned.

"Sit back down, Ridhan," Parth commanded. "Let's wait and see if this means a show."

The others murmured their assent. Ridhan slapped his stick against the ground. "Do we have to? We've got enough money."

Parth shoved a sharp silence into their midst. The others held their breath.

Finally, Nehal quipped, "Maybe we'll get so much money, we'll buy ourselves an elephant!"

It took a while before the first sighted villager noticed the elephant. The men listened as the rumor of its presence spread. Calls of "Elephant! Elephant!" steered the inhabitants toward the southern well.

"I knew it was an elephant," Ridhan said.

"Yes," Parth grunted. "But not a word about it now. You all know what to do."

They resumed their game, or rather pretended to, for they were no longer keeping score.

After an interval, three sighted girls came running up. "Uncles! We've got something to show you!"

"Ah, you darlings," Parth crooned. "Tell us, tell us what it is."

"No, no, no," the girls squealed. "We won't tell!"

"Aw," Nehal said, "but we're busy. Do we really have to go?"

As the six men approached the elephant, the villagers began to cheer. Parth signaled with his stick for his companions to start tripping and bumping into one another. He led them on a course that veered away from the elephant.

One of the girls shouted, "Not there! Let me show you!" She grabbed Parth's hand and took him to the elephant's side.

Parth bowed toward the girl. "Thank you ever so much, beautiful one!"

The five other men clustered around Parth, their arms, shoulders, legs, garments, and backs taking in the elephant. Nehal exclaimed under his breath, "It's much smaller than I thought it would be. The way the legends go on so, you'd think—"

One of the others agreed. "What a dud."

Ridhan whispered, "It's beautiful."

"Shut up," Parth snapped. "Time to work. I'll stay here. Nehal, you take the front. Ridhan, go behind."

The six men spread themselves around the elephant.

The crowd shouted, "What is it? We don't know! Tell us!"

A young man in the back of the crowd yelled, "Of course we know what it is. You blind men, it's an elephant!"

The crowd turned and hissed. Parth quickly boomed, "So it is, so it is. But we have never touched an elephant before. Let me see what it is like!"

He patted the elephant's front left leg up and down.

"It's a pillar!" he sang out.

The crowd laughed. Parth smiled and bowed. "Some pennies, dear friends?"

Several coins flew toward him.

"Thank you, our beloved friends. Now we shall hear what my brethren in darkness make of the fabled elephant."

The man standing behind Parth began swinging the elephant's ear.

"You're wrong!" he sang out. "It's nothing like a pillar. It's like a huge fan!"

The crowd laughed and more coins flew.

"Oh no!" sang out another man. "It's like a wall!"

"You blind fools!" sang out another, who was caressing the elephant's trunk. "It's like a tree branch!"

"You know nothing, nothing, nothing!" sang out Nehal. He kissed the tip of a tusk, gripping it as it moved. "It's like a spear!"

There was a pause. Ridhan, standing behind the elephant, hadn't said anything.

The crowd murmured, "There's one more. You, what is it like?"

Ridhan sighed. "All of this is—"

Parth shot back a warning.

Ridhan drew himself to his full height and held up the elephant's twitching tail. In a flat voice, he said, "It's a rope."

STUFFED CABBAGE MAN

by JULIE HECHT

SOMETHING BAD HAPPENED LAST year. Not like the really bad things that you see on the BBC World News. Not like the way it is now.

Somehow I got the idea to call the son of the people who used to live upstairs from us during my childhood. And he actually came to the phone. He lived in the richest part of California. I told him I was working on a family history. It included a part about his family when we all lived in a two-family house. Then we started talking.

But when we finished—well, we weren't really finished—he said he had to pay the lawn guy. I said they always sent a bill and a bookkeeper sent a check.

He was older, and retired, and he liked to just pay people after they did their work. He said he retired when he was forty, and I said, "Forty?"

"Yeah, I made millions. I didn't have to work anymore."

"How did you make millions?"

"Oh, in the tee-shirt business. You know those tee shirts with fake sequins on them that were popular for a while?" It was unfortunate that I pictured them.

"Yes, I do know," I said. "But I didn't know it was that lucrative."

Then he said, "Yeah. It was."

He sounded kind of like a tough guy. I forgot that he had a tough, rough quality underneath his cute face. And I remembered his mother often disapproved of his behavior, and he had caused problems when he was a teenager and even after that. She loved him anyway.

He said his mother kept asking him, "'Victor, tell me, really. How did you make all that money?'

Because she couldn't believe I could make that much money in the tee-shirt business." Maybe she thought he was in some kind of mafia. Some Orthodox Jewish gangster kind of thing. I guess there's no such thing. Maybe she thought he was in a drug cartel.

And I guess he had a great big lawn where he lived, in Beverly Hills or somewhere. I imagined it. Just a square green space with a chaise, something that looked like a painting by David Hockney. Oh, I didn't have to imagine, because I found his phone number on the internet, and they gave his address and it was in one of those neighborhoods. There was a lot to pay the lawn guy.

But the bad thing was, after the conversation was interrupted, he never called back. And although I hate email, I didn't want to interrupt him, so I sent him two emails asking if he would tell me more about his family. And I never heard from him again.

The family who lived upstairs from us was an older Orthodox Jewish couple. Their grown-up children no longer lived there. This was their son, who was now older than they were when I knew them. He said he was over eighty, maybe eighty-three. Maybe he told me, but I couldn't face it. So I don't know. I don't want to know.

Once, when I went upstairs, the father was sitting on a chair by himself right near the kitchen table and eating a bowl of stuffed cabbage. He was a kind of big man. Not tall. Just wide, probably from eating all that stuffed cabbage. His wife offered more and he accepted it a couple of times. He ate it without speaking a word. He stared at me in silence. His eyes looked light blue.

The daughter was married to a famous rabbi. I thought she looked like Ava Gardner. I once said to my mother, "You look like Ava Gardner." She said, "No, Joan Crawford." She sounded really annoyed. It had that how wrong and stupid tone to it. She told me that when she was in college and riding a bike, a male student called out and waved to her, "Hi, Joanie!" It must have come up before as a subject. She also told me that she had won prizes for the best legs. "I won prizes for my legs," she said many times.

The son was good-looking too. I don't know which parent or actor he looked like, because I was four or five and he was so much taller. I think it was the father but mixed with his mother. The father had a Russian, small-featured, ruddy face. The mother had somewhat tan skin and looked more like other people. The son must have looked like both of them. I didn't get to see the son's face unless he bent down to talk to me, or once or twice he lifted me up. Maybe my father lifted me up, too. It's a blur now. I know that when I was five he was already working, or maybe he was out of college, if he went to college.

The author

*   *   *

When we got to the school part, I asked, "Did you go to PS 161?" He said, "No, I went to the religious school." I never knew anyone that religious. He sounded scornful of public schools. Even disgusted. Maybe he was still Orthodox. Maybe he was remembering what it was like to be a child and a teenager in that era. There was no way to know they were Orthodox. They looked like regular people in America. They dressed the same way, maybe even better. They were all very well-dressed, but not too well-dressed.

I saw his sister mostly in the studio wedding photograph of her and her famous rabbi husband. The photo was kept in a gold frame on the piano. I never heard the piano played when we lived there. Maybe the daughter played the piano before we moved in, when I was a baby, and before she was married to the famous rabbi.

"My mother told me that your mother was married at age sixteen," I said.

"Fifteen," he said, as if this were a really important fact to correct. "She was married at fifteen. And had a baby at sixteen." There was a second of silence. It was obviously some kind of shotgun wedding. That was the first time it occurred to me. Because sixteen is not as alarming as fifteen.

Later in the conversation, he asked me why did I think of the past so much. I said, "Because the past is better." That seemed to annoy him. He sounded angry. Because he's had a full life, married three times, four children, lots of money he cares about, several Hollywood movies as he wanted.

His mother and mine once came to visit when I was first married. My mother wasn't good friends with his mother. It was some freak outing for something. They didn't have much in common, but she always told my mother unusual things about her family. My mother was the one who told me that his mother was married when she was sixteen.

My mother told me that Mrs. Werber would call Mr. Klein, a grocer who had a small vegetable market, and after giving him a phone order for vegetables, she would ask him to pick up some other thing from another store on the way with her delivery. "Isn't that something?" my mother said.

Anyway, they stayed married their whole lives. When she came to visit with my mother, she said, "He gave up his business and moved to Hollywood to become a movie star. Can you believe it? He had four children to support, and he wants to become a movie star. I don't know where he got the idea from." He was good-looking. Maybe he could act. When I was five and he was a grown-up, he used to bend down—he was wearing a leather bomber jacket—now I keep away from leather and all animal products—he used to joke around with me.

"Now I remember. You were always strange," he said. "You were really quiet."

"No, I wasn't. I was afraid." This was called just shy at the time. But maybe I was quiet because I was afraid. That's it.

"My older sibling was quiet," I said. "She was the weird one."

"Oh, yeah. The older sibling. I didn't really know her. Oh, now I remember you. That little shiksa face. I remember the whole family. Why weren't you a movie star?"

One summer, during the early teenage years, we were invited to visit his family. His parents were visiting them, and it was probably their idea to invite us. It was a neighborhood of Orthodox Jewish families in brick houses. We were living in our summer house in a nearby town.

I saw his wife in the hall in the back of the living room. She was putting the children to bed. She had her beautiful happy smile. He looked at me and shouted, "Hollywood! Eva Marie Saint! Grace Kelly!" Not true but a big surprise. It was more than a surprise, but less than a shock. Maybe it was a kind of shock.

This was a frightening scene. There were other actresses he included, but less shocking than those two.

His daughters were in my generation. He gave up his movie career and he retired when he was forty and just "lay" outside in the sun. I have a cringing feeling when people say "lay" instead of "lie." I've had several yoga teachers come here for lessons and say, "Now we're going to lay down on the mat." Almost all the yoga teachers, educated young women of the new world. In the beginning, I corrected them as politely as possible. Then the explanation became too much for me. After a while I gave up. But it was really hard to believe. A third-grade grammar mistake said over and over.

In any case, I told him how unhealthful that was, his lying in the sun, and he said he knew—he was at the dermatologist's all the time, getting things burned off. And then he gave up his movie career.

"Yeah, you were strange," he said again. But I didn't think I was strange. I said, "I was afraid. You were always joking and asking me if I was going to be a movie star." I hardly knew him. He didn't live there anymore. He only grew up there.

I sent him emails two more times. "Victor, I'd really like more information about your family for this chapter in my book. Is there any chance we could speak again?"

He didn't answer those two emails. Why? He'd said he didn't do anything but lie in the sun. Maybe he had other fun things he wanted to do. How would I know anything about his life.

He gave up his movie career. There he was. He was a cowboy in some movies. I didn't pay much attention to what the movies were. I just kept picturing him, lying out on a chaise in the sun in the Hollywood Hills. I pretended I knew that was a good place to live.

So he's on his third marriage. And he just lies on this chaise. I wanted to get him to tell me about his aunt Mitzi. I had never heard the name Mitzi. She wore a navy blue suit with a diamond pin, and she wore a small navy blue hat. Very elegant. Or medium elegant. He said she was his mother's cousin, not his aunt. Goldie was the aunt. I'd once heard Goldie Hawn in an interview say she had her aunt Goldie's candlesticks. She was in her tearful state when she said it. I understand why.

The woman named Mitzi was kind of what was called petite and had what was called a good figure. She was good-looking, too. She used to stare at me. She used to stare at me with this look, "Who is this little shiksa? Where did she come from?" Maybe she even said it. I knew that look from experience.

Of course I was quite observant, even though I was only four. She was always smiling a little wondrous smile when she looked at me.

Once I heard her say to Mrs. Werber, "That is the most beautiful child I have ever seen." I didn't take that seriously and thought it was said to all little children.

And then they'd get me talking. My mother had left me up there while she had an errand to do.

I guess Victor had a full life of wives and children and being a cowboy in movies. So he doesn't understand what I think. Plus, he's a multi-millionaire who lies on a chaise in the Hollywood Hills. I guess he doesn't understand why I'm interested in everyone who lived on our block. And he doesn't want to talk to me again. I mean, he's not a complete dummy. He said you get to a certain age and you start calling some of your friends from the past. That happened to him just last year. He called someone he had really liked and he found the person wasn't alive anymore. He sounded sad when he said that.

So maybe that's why he doesn't want to talk to me about the past. Because he likes the present and he likes to have fun.

His first wife was beautiful. Her name was Rickie. I remember when they first came to visit the Werbers, when she was expecting their first baby. And Rickie was wearing one of those navy blue suits people wore in those days. Maybe this was on the High Holy Days. She was smiling a beautiful happy smile. She had thick, dark brown eyebrows, perfectly tweezed to look natural. Or maybe they were natural. And she had shiny brown hair and bangs and her hair was cut short, like Audrey Hepburn's hair.

I said to him, "I remember when Rickie came to visit your parents, when you were having your first baby."

"Rickie died," he said. He sounded dark. His voice was low. I could hear the grief.

I said, "Oh no, when?"

"Just last year." More grief. On my side, too.

He sounded really sad. Even though they were divorced and he was married again, I guess he was remembering Rickie. Maybe he was reviewing his life's mistakes and that was why he just lay outside on the chaise. He remembered the early days of his first marriage. I guess that's why I'll never hear from him. Maybe I should try one more time. Or maybe the pain of not hearing from him is too much to bear. Because I really want to know about his family and I want to know about the people who lived on that block.

One thing he said was, "When you moved away to the suburbs, a Black family moved in. And guess what? My mother became best friends with this Black woman. They used to hug each other and throw their arms around each other." Now, that was news to me. I wished I had seen it. I tried to picture it many times. These are things I want to know about. But I don't know how to find out. I liked his way of describing it all. He remembered everything. Even though he had been in the sequined-tee-shirt business. He remembered the way writers do.

My father rarely spoke long with Mr. Werber. Mr. Werber used to treat my father as if my father were the landlord. He used to call my father and ask him to fix things. Not as a sign of disrespect, but because they knew he could fix everything. My parents thought it was funny when they first moved in. They would hear Mrs. Werber calling from upstairs. She'd be calling down the back stairs: "Mr. Hcccht!" And it was always that she just wanted him to fix something, even if a fuse blew. Mr. Werber—Murray—didn't fix anything. He just came home in his gray work suit and ate that stuffed cabbage.

But who knows, maybe they just ate it on a few occasions. I wasn't such a frequent visitor. Every time I went up there, it was fascinating.

She had two antique oil or gas glass lam kind they had in old movies. Maybe th with Ingrid Bergman, *Gaslight*. They had t crystal things that hang all around the lamp. I to touch them and make them clink together. She never told me not to touch them, or to be careful. She knew I was a careful child.

I remember the time my mother had to go out to do a short errand and brought me upstairs when Mrs. Werber was on the phone. She was on the phone for about half an hour. I was sitting there in a chair facing her from about ten feet away. During the conversation she put a wooden toothpick in her ear and twirled it around. We know it's bad to put even a Q-tip in your ear, especially after Father Guido Sarducci listed that as one of his new Ten Commandments. I remembered it as "Never put a Q-tip inside your ear, just around the outside." When I looked it up, I found out it read: "When you use Q-tips just go around the outside of the ear. Don't go poking in the canal."

When my mother came back and saw we were in the same positions she'd left us in, she reprimanded Mrs. Werber. "How could you leave her sitting there while you were on the phone all this time? Couldn't you give her something to do? A book, anything?"

I was surprised to hear her defend my situation. I didn't mind the sitting there. I was watching and listening. I couldn't forget the toothpick.

There were two girls who lived across the street and up the block. Their names were Mary Lou Loghren and Janie Herschliefer. None of us called her Mary Lou, we all called her Mary. Mary Loghren was from the only Irish Catholic family on the block. Others were plain American Protestants and Italian or Jewish doctors. Her father was a parochial school principal. He stood up really straight. He was tall and thin. Her mother was very thin and wore black dresses and her white hair was rolled up around to the back of her head with black hairpins. None of the other mothers had white hair.

Anyway, Mary Lou Loghren had two older brothers, Timmy and Jimmy, or names like that. They looked like boys in those short 1950s hygiene documentaries about washing your hands before eating dinner. They liked to tease us. One Halloween, we got dressed up as Elizabeth Taylor and Marilyn Monroe. We were about seven or eight.

Her meaner brother said, "Who are you supposed to be?"

And we said, "Elizabeth Taylor and Marilyn Monroe." She was Elizabeth. I was Marilyn.

He laughed. He said with a sneer, "You don't look like Elizabeth Taylor and Marilyn Monroe to me."

I always remember something that happened with Mary. We little girls were standing on the corner of the street where I lived, across the street from where Mary and Janie lived. It was a block closer to Ebbets Field—that direction. One of the girls pointed out the rim of Mary's cotton underwear slipping down an inch below her shorts. I was included in this terrible pointing out.

I could tell that it really hurt her, and she looked as if she might cry. She said her family couldn't afford to buy new underwear and she had to wear those. They looked normal. But I didn't think that her family was poor or different from any of our families, and today the underwear would be very stylish. Loose-rimmed, rib-edged underwear. Among my many regrets is that moment.

Mary and Janie were best friends. Janie's father was a doctor. They lived near an older lady who had a real Christmas tree at Christmastime. And she would invite us in for gingerbread. I didn't even know what gingerbread was, because they didn't eat gingerbread upstairs from us, where they ate that stuffed cabbage. I think they ate coffee cake.

The lady with the Christmas tree—I think she was lonely, because she was so happy to invite us in and give us the gingerbread cake. She was always happy to see us. We must have been really adorable girls. I think that cake must have been pretty good, but since I had never had gingerbread cake, I was afraid of it.

I remember Janie saying, "Go on, taste it. It's good." I think I stared at the Christmas tree in fear. We were allowed only little Christmas trees in our house. And they weren't real. They were toy Christmas trees. I don't think I'd ever seen a Christmas tree before that. I think I was five. Maybe we were all five.

It seemed that each girl was best friends with whichever one lived closest, like right next door. My best friend, Judy Lorber, lived next to us. A few of us would stand in the driveway and call, "Judy Lorber, can you come out and play?" I don't think I participated in the calling. I just stood there with my friends. Picture this.

From left to right: Unknown girl, Donna G, the author, Marion B

My father thought this was amusing. Four little girls standing between the driveways, calling up to Judy's house, "Judy Lorber, can you come out and play?" Sometimes he would repeat it a few times after he heard it. He was smiling. And then he would laugh, in between a chuckle and a laugh. He was happy. And those were his happy-family days with his children, before time led to events in the next decades. I know what only some of them were. It's a long list.

In grammar school I had a friend who told me her parents were divorced. I asked my mother what "divorced" was, and she explained. I asked where the children lived, and she said, "Well, where would you like to live?"

"I'd like to live with Dad."

"Why?"

"Because he likes me better."

"That's because he doesn't know what you're really like," she said.

What happened to the moments upstairs, with the cabbage family? Where are they? I wish I could see them. What about all those moments? And what about the ones downstairs, in our house?

Stephen Hawking would understand about time and memory, and could explain the subject. He understood infinity. It's a horrible thought. I can't think about infinity. It will drive me insane.

Where are all these things I'm remembering? They're still on my mind. What are the things that happened in the past?

I keep thinking of them, the cabbage man and

his family. Where is it, the past? It's not healthy to be thinking about scenes like that, especially in detail. I wish I had photographed it all, the way they did in the David Hockney documentary on the Smithsonian Channel. I didn't think of it. Of course, I was only four. I couldn't photograph it. I didn't know about holding on to the past and keeping the past. And so I'm doomed to write it. That must be why people make films.

Where is it? What exactly is it? Stephen Hawking or a neuroscientist-cosmologist could explain. You can't see it. It's gone.

THIS IS NOT MIAMI

by FERNANDA MELCHOR

Translated from the Spanish by SOPHIE HUGHES

IT WAS JANUARY AND the bitter wind whipped against Paco's bare face as he made his way down Montesinos toward the port gate. It was well past nine and the temperature was still dropping. That afternoon his father had predicted it would fall to as low as twelve degrees overnight, so Paco had thrown on a sweater and two work shirts before leaving the house: his tropical blood felt even that faint breath of the notorious norte wind.

He bought two cochinita pibil tortas outside the Morelos entry gate, then wolfed down two tacos from

Doña Almeja's stand: one with papa and chorizo, the other with papa and huevo, or "buebo," as the lady who served them pronounced it. Paco's shift began at ten and ended at six in the morning, but he was banking on the bad weather forcing them to suspend operations at the terminal. He'd be paid in full anyway, even if he put in only a couple of hours.

The wind prevented any loading and offloading of pallets and containers but it had no bearing on the work of the crew down on Dock 4, who specialized in loading cars for import and export. That night, Paco and the other guys working the night shift would be responsible for assembling and disassembling steel ramps and dragging them toward the haulers—also known as madrinas, because they carried the cars they transported in their immense bellies—attaching the ratchet tie-down straps that fasten the vehicles' tires to the ship, and then reattaching them to the trailers.

They were in luck. The supervisor had announced that there were only nine haulers to load before they could go home.

"We'll be out of here by midnight," said one of the crew, a man nicknamed El Burro, "the Donkey," who had a bulging gut and tattoos running the full length of both his arms.

Paco rarely worked Saturday nights but he was so deep in debt that he'd taken on a few extra shifts to make up for his splurging. As the youngest member of the dock crew, he was expected to work up in front. The others joked and chatted as they moved from strap to strap. They all had windburn on their faces, but none of them would have lowered himself to mention it, less still to wear a hat or gloves. Paco couldn't believe how rough and calloused the men's hands were—that's what his own hands would look like if he didn't hurry up and finish school, get a degree, and carve out a real future for himself, one that didn't depend on the physical strength that, little by little, would desert him.

And so, full of cheer and banter because they wouldn't have to wait until dawn to leave that freezing-cold quay, the men loaded eight haulers. The ninth one, however, still hadn't arrived at the terminal.

"There's been a delay," the supervisor shouted, to make himself heard over the wind. The last hauler had blown a tire in Tamarindo, fifty miles or so from the port. It was eleven o'clock and bitingly cold.

The dockworkers decided to sit on the ground, bunched together to protect themselves from the frigid, wet wind. They hadn't been resting there fifteen minutes when a blaze of red and blue lit up the darkness engulfing Dock 2.

"I smell trouble," muttered Chiles, an older man with gray hair and a potbelly. They called him Chiles on account of his last name, which was the same as a famous local brand of tinned chilies.

An immigration van and two pickup trucks packed full of special police officers careered along the esplanade and pulled up next to a small cargo ship moored to Dock 2. A federal police car with its siren on followed the pickups. Officers jumped down from the truck beds with their rifles raised, while others held police dogs by leashes, and they all boarded the vessel. Paco and his coworkers could make out only the narrow beams of flashlights being shone all over the deck.

"That boat must be packing a shit ton of drugs," Paco said. "The cops must have found..."

But he didn't get to finish his sentence, because

just then, amid much shouting and swearing, the police returned to the dock with about twenty more people, all of them black, as far as Paco could tell: skeletal men and women who were weeping and rubbing their bare arms and who vanished into the back of the immigration van. Some of the officers, confused as to why the dogs were still barking at the water, hung back by the side of the dock and shone their flashlights at the space between the ship's hull and the concrete wall, but after a while they also moved on.

By midnight, the port was once again deserted and Paco and his crew were still sitting on the ground awaiting the arrival of the ninth hauler. One o'clock came and went, then one thirty, and it wasn't until past two that the headlights of the last trailer emerged from the darkness of the terminal. The men made quick work of it and in a matter of minutes they were heading over to the supervisor to ask if they could leave.

"Hang on, boys. I'm just getting clearance," he said, holding his radio to his mouth as if he were about to eat it. "Give me an hour and I'll have you out of here."

Cursing the man and the mother who'd had him, Paco and the others parked their now frozen, aching backsides on the concrete floor. They entertained themselves talking about women, soccer, strategies to win the lottery, politics, religion, and women again. Bored and fed up, Paco let his mind wander as he gazed at the black sea through the gap between two rows of parked haulers. Suddenly he thought he saw something in that narrow space, a shadow gliding down, and he squinted to get a better look. His heart nearly jumped out of his chest when he finally recognized the outline of a man running toward them. Paco sat bolt upright and the others stopped laughing. For a moment he thought it must be a drifter, a junkie who'd somehow slipped past port security and was coming to mug them, but then he noticed that the man wasn't alone: a handful of equally ragged-looking figures were trailing him. While his fellow dockworkers got to their feet beside him, Paco counted nine men, nine black men, soaked to the bone, with their arms and legs covered in welts that looked like whip marks.

Paco moved toward the intruders with his fists raised, but the man at the front, the tallest among them, held up his open palms.

"My brother! Help me, brother, please, we're begging you!" he exclaimed in a thick Caribbean accent.

"Who are you?" Paco shouted back.

"We're Dominicans," the man said. "Please help us. We haven't eaten for a week."

"Don't give us away," the others whimpered in unison.

They were barefoot and stank of diesel and salt water. All of them were young, skinny yet strong, sinewy. They must have been clinging to the pier pilings for two hours, thought Paco, horrified. That's why the immigration police hadn't found them: the women and older ones hadn't been able to escape the hold, so they'd been caught, but these nine, the fittest among the group, the most desperate, had jumped into the water and clung to the barnacle-crusted concrete pillars, pounded by the raging waves and wintry gusts furiously sweeping across the port, until the police finally left.

Paco couldn't believe it.

"Please tell us we're in Miami…" another Dominican begged.

Paco gave a nervous snicker.

"Miami? You're kidding. You're in Veracruz!"

One of the men let out a sob.

"How much further to Miami?"

"Fucking ages, like three days by boat," Paco replied.

"And where are we?" another asked. "Where is Veracruz?"

The Dominicans started to glance furtively at the boat they'd just escaped from, as if trying to work out how to get back on it.

Paco drew the curve of the Gulf of Mexico in the air in front of him, then pointed to a space in the middle.

The Dominicans looked grief-stricken. It occurred to Paco that if they'd had sufficient liquid in their bodies, they would have broken down and cried like babies.

"And by land, how do we get to Miami?" asked the tallest man, the one who seemed to be the ringleader among the stowaways, the one who'd spoken first.

"I have no idea," Paco replied. "The furthest north I've ever been is Poza Rica."

"Help us, brother. Have mercy," another moaned.

Nine pairs of enormous yellowish eyes stared imploringly at the dockworkers.

"We'd better get these guys to the toilets," El Burro said at last. "If anyone sees them, they're fucked."

They led them to the bathroom in one of the warehouses. Once inside, Paco took out his remaining torta; he knew it wouldn't be enough to feed even one of those poor devils, but their hollow-eyed, emaciated faces were weighing on his conscience.

The ringleader snatched the roll so violently that he nearly took Paco's arm with it. He devoured half of it in two greedy mouthfuls, and on seeing the way his fellow sufferers were staring at him and salivating, he passed what was left of the torta to the closest one, a guy with bloodshot eyes who was dressed in just a T-shirt and some dark, tattered underpants. Another dockworker brought them some fresh water and the Dominicans literally threw themselves at the bucket containing the liquid; they drank with the desperation of people who have spent days at sea seeing nothing but the darkness of the hold, hearing nothing but the thunder of machinery, squeaking rats, and the murmurs of their fellow stowaways, who'd spent the whole journey praying that the captain of their vessel wasn't English or German; they'd been warned that some of the European officers were in the habit of tossing stowaways overboard, to spare themselves tiresome paperwork at their destination.

Once they'd all had a drink of water, the Dominicans proceeded to tell the dockworkers their story in hushed voices. A total of thirty of them had boarded the vessel, which was shipping wood from Puerto Plata to Miami. They'd bribed some of the crew to let them hide in the hold. Along the way they counted the stops they'd been told the boat would make: Rio Haina, Cristobal, Veracruz, and they'd prepared to disembark in what they'd believed was the United States. What they didn't know, however, was that they had made an additional stop, in Kingston, before sailing south to Panama.

One of the stowaways, who'd been silent until that point, walked up to Paco, took him by the arm, and pulled him aside a few feet from the group. His face was covered in insect bites.

"Brother, you have to help me. You don't know what I've been through. I have to get to the States. I have a sister there, in New York. She is waiting for me..."

He squeezed Paco's arm with his giant hand and spoke so close to his face that Paco could now clearly see the scars across his cheeks and forehead. Up close, the man's skin wasn't actually black, but closer to the color of buffed leather, reddish and oily, and the marks covering his face were a lighter shade of brown.

"My sister sent me a letter. She told me the men who killed my father are there. You don't know what I've been through, brother. My father owed people money and they killed him, they killed everyone when my sister and I were heading down to the river to collect water. You don't know what it's like to watch your father being hacked to death with a machete, to watch your mother being raped."

He howled through clenched teeth.

"They raped and killed her and I couldn't do anything as I hid in the bushes."

They're cigarette burns, Paco realized to his shock, unable to take his eyes off the Dominican's scars.

"My sister wrote to me. She said, 'Those guys are here, in New York,' and that's the only reason I'm going. I'm going to kill those sons of bitches. I'm going to hack them to death like they hacked my ma…"

Paco didn't dare say anything. So intense was the stowaway's hatred that Paco suddenly felt scared to go through with the plan that the other dock-workers and the hauler drivers—who were all still waiting for the green light to leave—had come up with. The idea was to hide the Dominicans inside the cabs of their vehicles and smuggle them out of the port, then let them out somewhere on the highway. This man was full of hatred, of murder-ous resolve, and nothing and no one was going to stop him. To reach his destination, he'd be capable of assaulting—even killing—a man, if he hadn't already.

One of Paco's coworkers—a dark-skinned man with curly hair and fine features, whom they nicknamed Thalía—rescued Paco from the pockmarked Dominican and led him out of the toilets and over to the quay. The wind had picked up and it smelled of burned grease from the boats.

"Listen to me, Ojitos. Don't you go giving that fucker your details," Thalía warned, his mouth practically touching Paco's ear to stop the wind from whipping away his words.

"No way. The guy's a psycho," Paco replied. He took a cigarette from the pack Thalía held out to him but couldn't get it to light. "Did you hear what he said to me? He wants us to help get him out, says he's got to go to New York to kill fuck knows who…"

Thalía patted him on the shoulder.

"Look, leave it to the drivers. They'll take them and kick them out somewhere near Puebla…"

"But how can we just let them into Mexico?" Paco shot back. "You don't know they won't kill or rape someone out there…"

In the distance, the hauler engines rumbled into action. One by one, they filed through the facility exit barriers.

"Remember what they say: sometimes even the devil needs a prayer…"

Paco had never heard that saying before. Knowing Thalía, he'd probably made it up on the spot.

From the other end of the concourse, the supervisor gave them the signal to leave.

As he wandered home down the still-slumbering streets, Paco went over the events of the night. It took him a couple of hours to reach his neighborhood on foot, because he saw no point in spending money on a taxi, and as he walked along with his hands buried in his pockets, the wind finally dropped and the dawn began to reveal itself in the reflection of the windows he passed. Paco spotted a lone little bird chirping away on a parched tree in the park near his house, and he watched as a glossy raven swooped down from a nearby cornice and snatched it in mid-flight before landing on the head of a statue to pluck the bird alive.

Sickened, Paco bent over to try to vomit up the torta, Doña Almeja's tacos, and the pint of bile that was already halfway up his throat. But for all his retching, he couldn't bring anything up: his throat had clamped shut. Wiping his brow with the tail of his shirt, he swore to himself that that was the last night shift he would ever work.

SCRAPS

by LEILA RENEE

"GIRL, THIS IS A KFC. Stop being dramatic," he's saying, while scrubbing my table with a rag. Rogue soap bubbles spray my face as he goes on. "You been sitting at this table for two days." He wipes his hands on his uniform shirt. "This is day three! You haven't brushed your teeth, bathed, nothing. You just sit here, feeling sorry for yourself. Why don't you look on the bright side? How you think I got promoted?" He gestures at his name tag: CHARLES III, MANAGER. "I manifested this."

"The bright side is blinding," I say, and sink into the booth as Charles III, Manager hovers over me. A headset pads his ears and muffled drive-thru orders blast from the earpiece. Webs of pink veins muddle his eyes.

"I already told you," I tell him. "I need time to think. This chick in China did it. Worked for her. Just a little longer. When I'm done, I'll leave."

"You keep saying that," says Charles. "And I get it. Breakups are trash. Last month my man left me for his coworker. But I looked on the bright side. If he left, he ain't for me. This dude wasn't for you. You know," he says, folding his arms, "you look just like my sister. Only she looks on the bright side."

"The bright side is blinding," I repeat, but Charles is already gone, picking up the next drive-thru order.

I feel bad. Charles has his own problems, being manager of this KFC in this neighborhood and all—which the top news station here in Milwaukee recently called "a Walmart-dotted wasteland." If I'm not the most depressed customer he's ever had, I'm certainly the most annoying. But I really do need time to think. I drove here two days ago for a sandwich. I sat in this booth and started to think about him. Then my thoughts rolled beyond themselves.

On our first date, two months ago, Joshua told me I looked 30 percent better in person and convinced me it does not matter how you die.

"Murder. Strangulation. Suicide. Ain't like we finna remember anyway," he said while we stood inside Kopp's Frozen Custard.

I was awed by his insight. And his height. Six foot three, according to his profile. My stomach throbbed with nerves, but I smiled.

He tipped the cashier 25 percent. I swooned at his generosity. On the way to his Charger, which was parked along a snowbanked road, he walked on the outer portion of the sidewalk. He opened the passenger door. A puddle of gray water had flooded the car mat. Flattered, I tiptoed inside and we cradled the hot bags on our laps. His car smelled like feet. I felt alive.

"So," he asked, fisting fries, "how many dudes you been with? What's your body count?"

"Two," I lied, mouth fizzing with Sierra Mist. It was more like that minus two. And this was my first date. After my father left, when I was seven, I saw my mother's anguish and swore off men for life. But then she had to go and ask me that question.

"I'm not gonna lie, Angel," Joshua said, smacking his food. "I been with a lot of people. Like, a *lot* of people. I'm not looking for nothing serious."

My heart churned with doom and delight. He was a walking petri dish, but at least he was honest. He would tell me everything.

I inhaled the thick air, smelling feet and beef. "That's fine." I half smiled, half nursed my stomach. "We can be casual, if you want."

"I just like the variety." He took a colossal bite. A bead of ketchup quivered on his lip.

"I get it."

"I *like* you." He marveled. "You're so understanding."

I felt my body inflate.

The windows fogged with heat and one-sided conversation. He talked about his job at Five Guys and how rogue oil burned him daily. He rolled up his sleeve and revealed a graveyard of scars.

Suddenly, he grabbed my neck, pulled me toward him, and planted a sopping kiss on my cheek. I glanced into the rearview mirror. I saw a ring of ketchup smear my skin like lipstick.

When he took a finger to carve a heart into the windshield, I took my thumb and rubbed its insides free of fog.

Charles III blinks. The pink veins contract and redden. Staticky customers shout from his earpiece. Charles has come to my booth these past two days near closing time, 11:00 p.m., begging me to leave. Sometimes, like now—day three—when the kitchen isn't crackling with oil or blooming with smoke, he sees fit to offer me relationship advice. He says he cares only because I look like his sister. And because he just got broken up with too.

Right now, however, he's pissed. He scowls at me like he's Colonel Sanders's evil twin, who for some reason is a gay Black man. Then he smacks his lips and hustles back into the kitchen, where two employees, Kiara and Devin, are assembling final orders.

The smell of bleach wafts over the registers. A pulsing beep punctuates the restaurant. No one comes in to sit during the day—just me and a few newspaper-toting elders who also don't want to be home all alone.

"Thanks," I call after Charles's retreating back. He gives a stiff thumbs-up. I slam my head onto the table and smell my onion breath. To my right is a wide window, and outside there's a weed-spiked parking lot and black dome of sky. I raise my head and inhale the stench of oil and chicken and blood. The overhead light, grotesquely fluorescent, drills into my eyes.

After a while, clacking footsteps come near. Charles wears his best loafers to work. "Two *years*," he'd said last night—my second, after I spread out on the booth to sleep and he passive-aggressively set a cardboard slab over my body. "I worked for two years to become manager. If you didn't look damn near exactly like my sister, I wouldn't entertain you. You're *lucky*."

The kitchen lights click off. The bulb above me dims. Charles edges closer. The silver upturned chair legs look like daggers.

The chairs didn't used to look so deadly. They used to be tulip chairs with circular bases. This location got a redesign a few years back. I know this KFC so well only because I ate here all the time as a child—it's not far from the West Side, where I grew up. Whenever my mother didn't feel like making dinner, she would visit this very drive-thru and get us—my father, little sister, and me—the same order: bucket of chicken, biscuits, potatoes. The night our father left—twelve years ago—she skipped the drive-thru and took us inside to eat. She said she was too sad to cook. That night, at a table just feet from this booth, I watched my mother drown herself in mashed potatoes. Her cheeks bulged like a chipmunk's. Her eyes glazed with want. My sister and I sat opposite her, each occupying a planet of our own. "Eva, Angel," our mother said to four-year-old her and seven-year-old me, potatoes sloshing her teeth. "Eat all your food."

That week we came here nightly. I ate the same thing every time: one drumstick, a scoop of macaroni, half a honeyed biscuit, and a spoonful of potatoes. The fourth seat of our table sat empty. We knew not to ask where our father was. We'd heard the screams beyond their bedroom door. We'd traced the swirling eyes of its wood.

On our sixth night, my mother filled my tray with potato peaks, ribbons of gravy, and flaccid coleslaw. I said I was full. She was dismayed. She could not comprehend how I could not feel empty.

I convinced myself that I did not miss my father. Not the snatch of his fingers when he pinched my cheek. Not the juicy turkeys he'd roast on Easter. Not the wooden scent of his Drakkar Noir cologne. I told myself I was glad he'd left. I no longer had to measure my footsteps, hide when he raged, or hear him sneak-flirting on the phone with women that weren't my mother. But my mother, like an idiot, missed him. On our seventh straight night here, my mother downed three drumsticks, a double-D breast, a sixty-four-ounce Sierra Mist, and three biscuits. Her biggest meal yet.

"Your dad," she said afterward, with an air of finality, "never loved us."

Eva cried wildly. I squeezed honey onto a biscuit.

My mom and I are nothing alike. Or very little alike. Sure, we're both BBWs. We both have a taste for cartoonishly awful men. And, apparently, we both love KFC. But besides those small points, we have little else in common. I go to college. She didn't. By the time she was nineteen, I was already two. I refuse to be like her. But back then we made a home out of those floor-bolted tables and tulip chairs that made the restaurant look like a hospital waiting room. Now this KFC is sleek: stainless steel, exposed brick, dagger-legged chairs. I remember Charles telling me, on day one, that managing this restaurant is his life's greatest honor.

Tonight, night three, he slides me a napkin-wrapped biscuit. But his nostrils flare with impatience. "One more night." He raises a finger, the nail caked with raw chicken. "*One*. I'm only being nice cause I know how it feels. If my district manager finds out about you, I'm done. She's gonna pop up for quarterly inspections any day now. You lucky our surveillance cameras don't work." He palms his mouth. "*Don't*"—his eyes flare—"tell anyone that."

Steam wafts from the biscuit. It entices me. Even though today I've already slammed two Crispy

Colonel Boxes. He drums his fingers on the table. I stare into the black bulb.

"What are you even thinking about?" He folds flour-streaked arms over his chest.

I unwrap the biscuit, break off a piece, set it soft and steaming on my tongue.

"I'm replaying everything. All two months. I think I missed some red flags."

"What was he, a friend with benefits?"

"Yeah. But still."

"Y'all were barely together two months? And you're this heartbroken?"

"I have attachment issues."

"Right."

Charles waves goodbye to Devin and Kiara.

"I thought he was good," I go on. "But he ended us via text. He didn't reply to my messages. It's like he killed me off."

"Angel," says Charles, checking his watch. "I feel for you. But I gotta close. I'll be out of here. It'll be quiet. You'll have plenty time to think about red flags or whatever you want to think about. Then tomorrow," he says hopefully, "you can leave."

With that, he returns to the kitchen. I put my head down, clutching the biscuit like a toddler. Minutes pass. A lock twists. Charles's red minivan reverses out of the lot.

Night means no beeping of machines, hum of faucets, or drone of customers. I lay my throbbing back on the booth's hard bench. My T-shirt sticks to my skin. My panties crunch. My period will start any day, since I stopped taking the pill three days ago, when Joshua left me.

This ain't gna work, read his text. *Your getting to attached.*

I'm sure my professors are emailing, wondering why I've skipped class. But my phone is a dead brick in my pocket. Still, I have to figure out what I missed, why I couldn't see this coming. Maybe my mom and little sister are worried, but it's not like I talk to them much anyway. Talking to my mom means being told all the ways I'm wrong. Talking to my sister means being told all the ways our mom is right. My sister is loyal to our mom because she's young and lives at home; she can't bite the hand that feeds her.

The cardboard blanket slips off me and flops under the table. I stare at the stained ceiling. Kisses of rust resemble eyes. One looks like a heart.

"I'm too big for condoms. Seven inches. They don't even make condoms that big," Joshua told me one week after we met, in another moment of what then seemed like refreshing honesty but now sounds like it would win gold in the red flag Olympics. "So you gotta get the pill," he said. "I wanna feel *all* of you."

I was flattered. I went to Planned Parenthood and got on the pill.

Two weeks after, he told me I wasn't wet enough, so I needed to drink pineapple juice.

I went to Pick 'n Save and bought organic pine-apple juice.

My mother had asked me, a few days before I matched with Joshua and he messaged that I was "beatiful," why I never had a boyfriend. She said that, yes, I needed to lose thirty-five pounds, but I still had good qualities and shouldn't be so alone.

She brought it up when I went to their place one night to help take down Eva's braids. "How come you don't have you a little boyfriend or nothing?"

"Because I don't wanna end up like you," I said bitterly.

She smacked her lips and waddled away.

A few days after that, her question playing in my mind, I made a Tinder profile. I resolved to find a boyfriend and show her how the whole "love" thing was supposed to be. See how it was supposed to feel.

The biscuit on the table is hard now. I touch it and it crumbles through my fingers. I lie flat in the booth. My tailbone aches. I can't get up. The pain anchors me. My levee breaks. It spreads hot and wet along my bottom.

After a while, a warm spot grows cold.

"Angel, what in the hell?" Charles stands over me all incensed, his keys in one hand, a McDonald's coffee in the other. The restaurant echoes with emptiness. Kiara and the others mill about in the kitchen. I yawn as the morning sun glows through the window. Charles gapes at the puddles in the seat and on the floor, at the dark spot outlining my crotch. My chest burns with shame. And heartburn. I've been eating too much chicken.

"Did you really—" Before finishing, he runs to the back and emerges with a mop and a spare pair of khaki uniform pants.

"I'm so sorry."

"Clean it," he orders, teeth clenched. "Now. Ten thirty. We're opening. I just got here. I can't believe they didn't wake you up." He points to his employees. "What if Sheila comes today? How am I gonna explain you all camped out here?" He holds my eyes in his.

"Sheila?"

"The district manager!"

"Joshua told me he was a ho," I tell Charles. "And his car smelled like feet."

"You still talking about dude? After all this?" He swings the mop. Tangles of hair cling to its tentacles. "Clean!"

"I just want you to know last night wasn't a waste. I got good thinking done. I didn't have an epiphany yet, but I realized some things."

Construction workers stream through the door and scoff at the smell of chicken and pee.

Charles eyes me with bewildered fatigue. And pity. "My ex," he says, with frantic resignation.

"Same thing. He was trash from the jump." He speaks as if he's off the clock. "Same week we met, we got chlamydia. He said I gave it to him. But looking back, *he* gave it to *me*."

"Damn."

"Yeah." He hands me the mop and the pants. "Go change," he says. "Then clean."

Later, Kiara gifts me a bucket of disfigured wings. The lunch rush has passed, and the restaurant inflates with the quiet between lunch and dinner.

"Thanks." I lift one that looks like a human hand. "But I shouldn't. I'm big enough."

"Big? Please. You just thick." She sits opposite me.

"Tell my mom that. She's bigger than me but always going on about how I—"

"So anyway," she says, twirling her eyebrow ring. "Who was this dude? Charles told us some stuff, but not everything."

"I don't even know. I thought he was good. He took my virginity. I know he had a dark past, but, like, I been through stuff, too, and—"

"Girl." She squints. "This is a KFC."

"Sorry."

"Heartbreak." She shrugs, staring out the window into a flock of gulls. Shrieking caws permeate the glass. "Life." She shrugs again.

I study a pile of half-eaten chicken wings in the middle of the parking lot. A bird stabs its beak into the flesh. Kiara floats back to the register. The booth feels somehow emptier.

Not for long. An old white lady, who for some reason still lives in this neighborhood, rises from her table and places a veiny hand on my shoulder.

"Heard about your predicament," she says. "Well, overheard."

I snap a wing in two.

"Heartbreak," she says, "is like a camera. At first, you're zoomed in. Day by day, you zoom out. Till you see the whole picture. That's when perspective comes. And that's when"—she laughs—"you're over the joker!"

"Thanks." I chew.

"Takes a while to pan out, though."

* * *

Before tonight's dinner rush, Charles joins me as I eat my last wing.

"Any progress?" he asks, then mixes coffee and Pepsi in his McDonald's cup from earlier and takes a horrifyingly casual swig. "You reached your 'epiphany'? Can you leave now?"

"I just don't know why I let my guard down. When I got around Joshua, it's like I turned into a little girl again. It's like I *reverted*. I should have known better. I—"

He plants his face onto the table. A dime-sized bald spot crowns his head.

"I'm sorry, Charles. For being annoying. I just don't have anyone else to talk to."

"Thinking's different than doing. I read the employee manual four *times* before my first day, and still I couldn't bread the chicken to save my life. Sheila trained me that day." He glows with nostalgia, then grimaces. "And maybe she didn't come today. But she could tomorrow."

I throw the clean bone into the box. "I'm so dumb."

"No," he snaps. "You were just dickmatized.

Don't you go to college? Matter fact, don't you have class?"

"I can skip a few days. UWM. Psych major. See. I should have known better."

He laughs. I don't.

"I wanna go back to school."

"For?"

"Something corporate. Get outta Milwaukee. Heard Kentucky ain't so bad. That's where headquarters is. I'm tired of this city. I feel so..." He mimes wringing his neck.

"Suffocated?"

"Suffocated," he says. "Even my mom wants me to move somewhere bigger. Better."

"I wanted to go to school out of state, but my mom wouldn't let me."

"Where's your dad?"

"Green Bay. Last I heard."

I wonder if anyone ever asks my father, *Where is your daughter?* I wonder what he says in response.

A line forms at the register. Charles flashes a determined grin and adjusts his headset. With Charles gone, I exhume another memory: the night before our five-week anniversary. Joshua and

I were lounging in bed, our damp bodies tangled in my sheets. His heart thumped against my back as I licked the burned flesh of my mouth—courtesy of yet another pineapple juice overdose—and wondered why we only interacted horizontally. All his texts to me read, *Can I cum over tonite?* 👀 😏 I couldn't tell if he liked me or if he just genuinely needed a place to sleep.

"How do you feel about me?" I asked him. My room grew darker. He propped himself up on his pillow, digesting the question.

"You cool," he said.

"Cool," I tell Charles now, during his break, after the dinner rush. He joins me in the booth. Just to rest his legs, he claims. I think Charles secretly cares about me. Why else would he let me stay? Kiara's fly-swarmed gift sits finished on my table. Purple trails shadow the evening sky. Engorged gulls stumble across the lot. Customers wander inside. I pray none are Sheila.

"He just said 'cool,'" I tell Charles, who takes a weary gulp of his Pepsi-coffee.

"Well, go on," he says with restraint. "What you say back?"

"That I was happy. I hugged him."

Charles cringes.

"I know." I hang my head. A linty braid skims my forehead. I perk up. "But maybe I can text him from your phone? He blocked me. Maybe I can ask about his trauma? His dad wasn't in his life either, and—"

"Angel."

"Sorry."

Charles softens his face into one of unexpected pity. "What did you even *like* about this dude? He sounds like a parody of a fuck boy."

I start to tell him. But it makes my eyes burn, so I change the topic. "What did you like," I ask, "about your ex?"

He tents his hands beneath his chin. "Hm." He twists his mouth to one side. "I think I just didn't want to be alone. If"—a wistful look lines his face—"I'm being honest."

"Maybe it was that." It spills out. A million needles prick my eyes. "Maybe Joshua was the first man to ever want me. Even if it was halfway."

Charles's face breaks. "Oh, Angel," he says. "Don't cry."

Charles leans over and palms my back, and I feel my fat jiggle at his touch. The touch transports me.

"Fat ass," my father had barked from down the hall. I watched my mother pretend not to hear him. Later that night, she cooked dinner for us— for him with a blank face. Eva and I sat at the kitchen table amid the sizzle of Hamburger Helper. He entered the kitchen wearing a pleather jacket and the tinted sunglasses germane to 2002. "I'm going out tonight," he announced. My mother started to ask where, but the door slammed behind him.

We three ate dinner in silence. The ellipses of his absence floated between us.

The following morning, my mother got my sister and me dressed for school. I hadn't heard him come home the previous night. Still, on our way out, headed toward the staircase, I saw a plate of untouched leftovers she'd left out for him. How could she fix a plate for someone so awful? My mother's subservience filled me with rage.

Charles's palm digs into my spine.

I lift my head. It spins.

"What?" Charles eyes me, aghast. He panics, looks over his shoulder. "Sheila?"

"Nothing."

He pats my hand and returns to the kitchen, leaving me alone.

"He said he cheated because he needs variety. Can you believe your father?"

When Charles leaves the booth this time, I let myself remember how my mother said this twelve years ago. My little sister and I watched her rant about this during our eighth straight dinner at KFC at a table stacked with containers of stiff gravy and crusted potatoes. Eva sat beside our mother and clung to her every word. I sat opposite them and flossed a plastic knife through the newfound gap in my teeth. I had just lost my front tooth an hour earlier while biting into a biscuit, and my mother had wrapped the tooth in a napkin for the tooth fairy. "You have to make a wish tonight," she said hollowly.

I ran my tongue over the swollen flesh. I relished the metallic tang.

"Look," she said. "I'm sorry I'm telling y'all this, but it's best to know the truth about your dad." A sad look colonized her face. She stared at the bloody napkin.

"Will we ever see him again?" Eva asked in her baby voice.

My mother gave a faint shrug. "Last I heard," she said, her eyes cadaverous, "him and the chick are moving to Green Bay." She and Eva wrapped their bodies into a wailing knot.

I blinked and wondered what to wish for that night. Unwrapping the napkin, I studied my tooth. It was difficult to believe I could produce something so hard, so solid.

"Why," I said, breaking my facade of indifference, "do y'all even *care*? He was *mean*."

My mother dropped her biscuit. My sister spit out her Pepsi.

"When you grow up," my mother said, with contempt, "you'll understand."

I tongued the black hole in my mouth.

*　　*　　*

Two hours pass. I don't notice Charles is next to me until he screams my name. I can still feel the tooth stabbing my finger. I hear jingling keys.

"I'm out." He wags the ring. The restaurant is dark. "Come on."

"Please."

"What *now*?"

I touch his arm. The skin is warm.

"I can't go back," I say. "My place reminds me of him."

Charles collapses into the seat. "Angel. I'm not your therapist. Nor your 'magical Negro.'" He points to his name tag. "Does this thing say, 'Michael Clarke Duncan'?"

"Tonight's the last. Promise."

"You're young," he says, rolling his eyes. "I don't know why you put so much pressure on yourself."

"Now that I think about it, I settled. For the bare minimum. For"—I point to the bucket—"scraps."

A fly orbits the rim. I whack it dead.

"Hindsight is twenty-twenty." Charles yawns. He gathers the fly in a napkin and its wings crunch. "You don't always know the red flags. If that were the case, I would've known my ex had chlamydia."

He adjusts his headset and swirls the liquid in his cup. A black splash wets the table and creeps toward the pile of crumbs. "Where's your car parked?" he says. "I'll walk you out."

"One more night? Please. I'm so close to an epiphany. And I never asked you to give me advice. I was perfectly okay sitting here alone."

"In *my* restaurant. Right before *my* quarterly inspection."

I watch the crumbs swell and soften in the puddle. Over his shoulder, Kiara smokes a cigarette out the drive-thru window.

Charles sets down the cup. Stares into its bottom. "I guess when you're starving," he says, sighing, "you'll eat anything."

"I thought you were over him."

"I am," he snaps. Recomposing himself, he says, more quietly, "I am."

"Are you?"

"Angel, let's not do this. You're the last person I'd come to for a therapy session. No offense."

"But I'm a psych major."

"Yeah." He laughs, and sweeps his arms across the restaurant and toward the gravy stains on my shirt. "And look where that got you." He sighs. "Work is good. It keeps me busy. Plus, I've got business to take care of. I help pay my sister's tuition."

Kiara shuts the drive-thru window. A row of lights flickers off.

"Where's your car?" Charles asks, yawning.

I point out the window and feel my arm jiggle. I have got to stop eating those Crispy Colonel Boxes.

"Come." He rises. "I heard through the grapevine that Sheila's most likely coming tomorrow."

"My mom used to come here," I blurt desperately. "Twelve years ago. We came here."

Charles darts his eyes. "For real? Is that why you came here? Some psych experiment?"

"Don't be ridiculous. I just wanted a sandwich."

He squints.

"We used to sit at a table in the middle."

"Before the redesign? Man, you're lucky. That was really an era. I would have killed to see it. It's crazy how much KFC is devoted to improving the customer experience, you know?"

"Sure."

The corporate glaze flees his face. "Wait." He regards me. "Your mom know you here?"

"Four days of silence is nothing new for us."

"She's probably worried. Your sister too. My mom flips if I don't call at least twice a day."

"All my sister ever does is make TikToks that get eight views. And me and my mom are nothing alike."

"Oh really?" he says, all smug. "Then why are you here?"

The crumbs have gone soggy and pale.

Charles rises, palms my shoulder, and walks away.

Later, before his van leaves the lot, I see his slumped silhouette in the front seat. His head rests on the steering wheel. He no longer looks like a manager. He looks like a man who has to go home alone.

With tomorrow's heightened chance of a Sheila cameo, I oil the wheels of my mind. I don't want Charles to get in trouble. I don't want to add to his plate.

I force myself to recall the last night that Joshua and I spent together—one week ago today—when I cooked him dinner for the first time ever. I could feel him drifting away. I wanted to lure him back to shore.

But when he got to my place, he said he wasn't hungry.

After he left that evening, my body still throbbing from his touch, I fixed him a plate. Just like my mother had done. I figured he'd eat it later, the next time I saw him.

The crumbs are dry come morning. Charles isn't in yet. The sun seeps through the window, bathing the empty restaurant rose gold. I rise, stretch, survey the damage. Stains and stench cloud my clothes. Biscuit crumbs carpet the table. I cup my hands, brush the crumbs in, and turn to go.

But it doesn't feel right. To leave like this.

I fan the crumbs back onto the table. Arrange them into letters:

THANKS AND SORRY

An echo of footsteps. A creak of opened door.

And now, as I start my car, the light through the windshield is like a revelation.

It's only here, in my car, driving home with the sun nearly blinding me, that I let myself remember a moment when it seemed my mother was doing the best she could. The last night we returned home from KFC, I slid my tooth under my pillow and wished for my father. I wasn't sure if I was wishing that he'd come back, or that he'd just be better. I finished my wishing and was pretending to sleep when I heard my bedroom door click open. A shard of light sliced my room. My mother shuffled in and set her cheek on my chest. She said nothing. I put my palm on her head. With every breath I took, she rose and fell. On her neck, I smelled my father's cologne.

I hugged her, savoring the softness of her body. She held me like I was someone who would never let go.

After a few minutes, she started sniffling, rose, and left my room. Once she was gone, I clutched the tooth and changed my wish. I wished that we were still hugging.

At a stoplight now, I want to turn and drive to her house. To kneel at her feet and tell her I am sorry for thinking she was the kind of person I was too rational to ever become.

I plug my phone into the car charger. An influx of messages. None from him. But one DM on TikTok from Eva—a video of her wistfully lip-syncing to Rihanna's "Where Have You Been." Ninety views. Eva's youth shines brighter than ever. I see her eyes' childish glint and am at once startled by the fact of my seniority—by the fact that older sisters are supposed to be there for younger sisters. By the fact that I, in my self-pity, have not been.

And I see twelve texts from my mother, asking if I'm okay.

As the stoplight glows green, I press the accelerator and resolve to text her back. Later, of course. Once I'm off the road. She can't stand texting and driving. And later, when she inevitably answers my text with a call—her "Angel, where the hell have you been?" tinged with relief—I'll return her call and tell her that we have a lot to talk about. More than I ever thought.

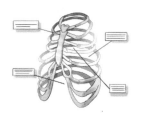

TRUE, FALSE, FLOATING

by MEL KASSEL

ALL FOUR OF THEM are holding champagne flutes. The receptionist asks, and they assure her that the glasses are empty props.

"I'm marrying a doctor," declares Allie. "I know not to drink before anesthesia."

"I have to check! I'm sorry." The receptionist searches for an understanding face, but their judgment is collective and irreversible. They're wearing mock-silk pink sashes across their torsos that read ALLIE HAS IT ALL! in purple lettering. The sashes look absurdly official at this hour, the receptionist thinks. She pushes consent forms across the desk to each of them.

"I'm starving," Georgia says. Her signature is the most curt, a jagging of upward lines. She bears down hard with her pen each time and flips the pages so they almost tear free of the staple. "Can my emergency contact be one of them?" She points her pen at the other three women.

"Well, they'll be here with you, so I don't know if—" the receptionist begins, but she stops herself. "It can be whoever you want."

Phoebe's signature is practical, legible, squat. She tucks a coil of hair behind her right ear as she signs. With her left hand, she rubs Allie's back in rapid circles. She doesn't read the forms, just finds the next blank line and fills it out. When Georgia pretends to cheat off her, raising her head over Phoebe's shoulder, Phoebe cocks her hip and bumps her friend away.

"She's *frisky* in the morning," Georgia says. "Ooh-la-la."

Danielle's signature looks like swooping calligraphy. She reads some of the fine print, frowning.

"If we aren't satisfied with our readings, there's not even a partial refund?"

"Unfortunately, no. Although we do offer a discounted second reading in those rare cases."

"So if we don't like getting cut open the first time, we can get cut open again?" Danielle laughs, then looks to either side for support. Everyone has their head bowed over their forms. They have to sign in several spots.

Allie's signature flatlines after the large belly of the cursive *A*. It looks like a child's balloon at rest on the floor. Seeing it, the receptionist makes a last grab for goodwill.

"Are you taking his name, or—"

"I'm taking it," Allie says, her face bright and cold, her eyes fixed on the paper.

Cowed, the receptionist busies herself with the computer and waits for them to put down their pens.

Six more weeks and she'll be able to exchange vacation time for a reading of her own. She feels against her smock for the bulge of a rib, sighs. These women. They do not have to walk so slowly up to the edge of change, consider its height, find the safe way down. The receptionist sees the Ospex during every shift and has yet to be addressed by name. But these women's faces and names are on flash cards—she's watched the Ospex before appointments, practicing, shuffling, muttering. You can call and get your face on one of those flash cards the same day, if you're rich. Otherwise, you go on living zipped-up, a box unable to open itself.

The Ospex likes to say that everyone is their own oracle. The receptionist believes this, or she wouldn't work here. But money can't be the only thing that makes someone worth opening. Why shouldn't everyone know what's inside themselves? Who wouldn't benefit from the revelations? She's seen so many readings, and she still thinks each is beautiful and raw, humbling by necessity, but empowering, too, if you know how to grow from it.

She'll start her own clinic one day, and she'll charge clients on a sliding scale, income-based. She'll be able to afford it because her readings will discover those geniuses untouched by luck. She'll invest accordingly. She has it mostly planned out. When she gets her reading, she's going to ask for a focus on the fifth true rib, the one for career.

*　　*　　*

They have to sit in the windowless lobby while the staff prepares. The receptionist gives them gowns to change into—thin white cloth instead of the rough paper Georgia had anticipated. She unbuttons the panel that covers her torso and lifts it up to flash the group.

"Gimme your beads, bitches!"

Allie cackles and Phoebe shakes her head, stuffing her champagne flute and sash into her purse. Danielle makes anxious pushing motions with her hands.

"Cover up," she hisses.

"No one else is coming in. Relax, Danny, or they'll charge you for extra sedative." Slowly, so Danielle knows it's not a full victory, Georgia buttons the panel back in place.

The four of them sit on the lobby's only couch, facing the huge black horseshoe-shaped desk. The receptionist has to tap along the inner curve with her feet to roll her chair from monitor to monitor.

She's too prissy for a desk that size, Georgia thinks. It looks like it's about to gobble her up.

"Okay, who's going first?" Allie asks. "We might have to flip coins. Unless someone actually doesn't want to see a reading?"

Obviously, Allie will be last. She'll get to see all of them peeled back, all of them drooling, and no one will be left to be a live audience for her. She deserves that dignity. But they'll get tiny flash drives with footage on them, and they've planned to watch the video of her reading after dinner the following day, when they're allowed to get drunk again.

"I'd like to see a reading," Danielle says.

Georgia and Phoebe don't know Danielle. She's a friend of Allie's from college, now in consulting. But from the moment they all converged, squealing and embracing on Allie's porch, Georgia could sense how easy it would be to make her uncomfortable. Definitely type A, an animated pencil skirt. She thinks she has something to prove, or at least something to preserve, in the face of Allie's much-older bonds with Georgia and Phoebe. She's already cast herself as a more righteous alternative. Like, stick with her and you'll actually get somewhere.

"I'm sure we'd all like to see a reading," Phoebe says. Georgia rolls her eyes at her friend's serene teacher-voice. "But someone has to go first. And we can all watch the videos later."

"Let's flip a coin, then," Allie says.

"Wait, look." Georgia clasps her hands together and pauses, settling on the right words, exhaling. She turns to Danielle. "We haven't seen Allie in a while, and she's been staying with you. This is definitely shitty of me to ask, but would you mind going first? I just feel like it would be nice to have some trio time, and then we all regroup for the rest of the week, and no one's feelings are hurt?"

"That *is* shitty, Georgia." Phoebe puts a hand on Danielle's shoulder. "You don't have to say yes to that, unless you want to."

"No, of course she doesn't," Georgia adds. She stares at Danielle, who seems to have frozen, her eyes flicking between the two of them.

"Just flip a coin, guys. It really doesn't matter to me." Allie stretches her arms behind her head and leans back. The light from the candles makes her blond bangs look like shimmering filaments, a fairy veil. She's shorter than all of them by a head.

Georgia remembers her saying that the accident had stunted her growth—they'd had to fuse some vertebrae. There's a skin graft, too, hugging her calf, where the muscle doesn't work as well. She's twice as likely as any of them to suffer a fall. You can see the difference in her steps if you're looking for it, how she's in a quiet hurry to get off her left side.

We were all so stupid then, Georgia thinks. That word, aimless and animal, is the most fitting. Sometimes, Georgia tries to probe inside herself to see if it's still there, the chuckling, stupid meanness that had once rolled off them inexhaustibly, like sweat. She never finds it at the same concentration, and she's relieved.

Before they can reach a decision or find a coin, the door behind the desk opens and the Ospex comes in. She's wearing white scrubs, pants so billowy they're easy to mistake for a skirt, and a white surgical cap. Georgia recognizes her hands from the photos on the website: short but widely spaced fingers, small palms, perfect for "minimizing invasiveness, maximizing sensitivity." Allie chose her because she's the only one in the city who reads ribs ungloved.

"Allie," she says. "Congratulations."

She swishes toward them, takes both of Allie's hands, pulls her up into a hug. She moves her hands to Allie's shoulders when they separate.

"Well, you have a very open cage. It really breathes. I can tell you that much already." Her voice is surprisingly stern, not at all husky.

"We were trying to decide who should go first," Phoebe says. Georgia thinks her gambit has worked, that Danielle is about to volunteer; there, she's raising her chin and opening her mouth, if everyone would just be quiet—but then the Ospex nods at her instead.

"Let's start here."

"What? Why me?"

Is she being punished? Had she been too rowdy before, trying to make Allie laugh with her Mardi Gras bit? Had the Ospex heard them pressuring Danielle?

"It has to be someone, and you look ready," the Ospex says. Crafty of her to work in the compliment. If Georgia complains, she's not game.

There's no psychic jolt when the Ospex takes her arm, no inexplicable hypnotizing warmth. But that's fine; Georgia isn't a true believer. She tenses at first, moves to wheedle Danielle one last time, but Allie looks so pleased to be getting started. She's smiling at Georgia, proud.

Georgia achieves peace by reminding herself that this day is for Allie, not for them. Something fun and expensive and harmlessly mystical. Whatever Allie wants. She's always asked for so little, despite the fact that she's entitled to something huge. Even after this, Georgia will still owe her.

She holds her fear under her loyalty and drowns it there. She pictures Allie's skin graft, remembers Allie explaining how the sweat glands there don't work, how that part of her leg gets hot all the time.

"Is that okay, Georgia?" Allie asks, and Georgia nods, turning her head as the Ospex takes her away so her friend can see her smile back.

The receptionist leads the three remaining women into the viewing room. She has them pick their chairs from the array lined up against the back wall, all of them leather and dyed in nonthreatening pastels. Allie selects lavender, Phoebe pink,

Danielle mint green. They don't volunteer to help her as she waddles backward three times, arms straight and elbows locked, dragging each chair to the middle of the room by the bar under its foot-rest. She knows her face is flushed when she stands up and gestures for them to sit. They must think she doesn't mind this at all. They aren't getting their floaters read, but she'd stake money on short, skinny bones with all the pockmarks of selfishness.

"Thank you," Danielle says, at least.

Allie takes the middle spot, and the reception-ist notices for the first time that there's something odd about the way she moves. She can't place the center of the peculiarity, but she doesn't want to stare, especially now that Danielle is staring at *her*, her jaw working from side to side, her expression forbidding. Phoebe, meanwhile, looks through the huge window into the reading room. Both of them wait until Allie is seated before sitting themselves.

"There's a smaller, soundproof room through the door on your right in case anyone wants a break, and believe me, there's no shame in that at all." The receptionist doesn't mention the lidded bucket in the room. If she had to guess which one of them might puke, though, she'd pick Phoebe, who has paled a bit and started to tug at the leather on the arms of her chair. "Any questions?"

They shake their heads and she leaves them, thankful. She's used to comforting clients, addressing their worries, which are almost always about residual pain or waking up during the reading itself. She likes to quiet them. She's been told she's very soothing without being too condescending or motherly. But she doesn't think her scripts will work on these women—they wouldn't listen. They're frantic in a way that doesn't want to be touched. The readings will be so good for them.

The team wheels an unconscious Georgia to the center of the reading room and mumbles about her vital signs. The Ospex enters last and stands behind Georgia's head, facing the window. Everyone wears white. They move as if each of them had just recalled a new stage position, suddenly stepping over to adjust a dial or ready a tray. They seem to emanate a soft glow, disrupted only by the slices of pink skin above their masks, below their caps.

"The white outfits are so we can see the blood," Allie says. "The Ospex said it's respectful, so we can appreciate what goes into the reading. I could have chosen darker scrubs, but..."

"I like that," says Danielle. "Otherwise it would feel like they were sugarcoating something, or like they thought we couldn't handle it."

"I'm still not sure if I can handle it," Phoebe says. She's blinking a lot and keeps gathering her curly hair in both hands, combing through it with her fingers.

"It's okay if you can't," says Danielle. She prays that Phoebe will slink into the side room as soon as the first bit of blood wells up. She thinks about what she could say to Phoebe later this week, maybe when they're both in line for the bathroom at one of the clubs Allie wants to go to, something like *Guess you're pretty squeamish now, huh?*

It's a petty fantasy. She'd never. And she doesn't need to—Danielle has faith that the Ospex will expose Phoebe and Georgia in a much more conclusive sense. The clinic advertises unbiased, stream of consciousness–style readings. No edits, no coddling, and, therefore, "the best betterment."

Danielle knows about the accident: how, in sophomore year of high school, Georgia and Phoebe claimed a Ouija board could connect Allie with her dead father; how they pushed the planchette and pretended he was reaching out; how the board instructed her to close her eyes and cross the same highway he'd crashed on; how she, small and pawing at the false link, had done it; how a car had swerved but still clipped her.

Danielle imagines Allie spinning away from the car, her back splintering on the inside. At what point had her hope collapsed? Right then? Later, in the hospital? Only after the girls copped to the lie?

Phoebe and Georgia had apologized. Allie had accepted. When Allie told the story, she made it sound like their friendship had never been in jeopardy. She made fun of herself. She said things like "I mean, all high school girls are fucking sociopaths."

Danielle had let her horror be known, had let it be laughed off. But she's been waiting ever since to meet these women. And, yes, to push for a reckoning.

There's no pause or announcement to mark the transition into surgery. Everything proceeds at the same casual speed. Someone opens Georgia's gown, and for a second it seems like the skin beneath will keep rising up and spread out like dough, but it's only Georgia breathing in.

"They're going to do it," says Allie.

"Oh god." Phoebe covers her eyes with a hand. Danielle bites her lip.

The blade sinks two vertical lines into Georgia, each line about six inches long, starting below her armpits and ending below her breasts. Two people move in with suction tools that look like long drinking straws. Blood shoots through the straws so redly it seems like it should make a noise in the hueless room, a whistle or a moan.

"Okay, it's not so bad." Phoebe has opened her eyes and is reassuring herself. Danielle can hear her regulating her breath.

"Soon it'll be us in there," she says, looking at Phoebe, wanting her to know that she knows.

"Shh," says Allie.

All of them lean forward as the Ospex bends over Georgia's face. She doesn't acknowledge the window. She brings her hands to the cuts, splays her outer fingers and thumbs across Georgia's skin, presses gently. Her middle fingers slip inside and her mouth opens.

"Fifth true pair," she says. Her voice reaches them through speakers mounted in the corners of the room. "Career, finances, public self. Surface: largely smooth. Costal grooves: shallow. A good career, fulfilling for her, if a little demeaning in the eyes of others."

Danielle can see the raised flesh travel where the fingers are scanning. They're in up to the first knuckle, then the second, traveling along the rib. She looks at the Ospex, then at Allie, back and forth, not wanting to miss any developments in either place. She knows that Allie is a believer. At the tentative beginning of their friendship as college freshmen, during the conversations about tarot cards and rising signs, neither of them had wanted to tip their hand, lest the other think her crazy. But slowly, again and again, they found themselves on the same level. They invented customized card spreads in their dorm rooms, went to calculus together the next day. They could fit both systems inside themselves without itching at the paradox.

"Long-bodied ribs. The cartilage seams are straight. No hiccups for her on the corporate ladder, if she puts in the effort. Very straightforward reading. A good opener; I like that very much." The Ospex doesn't smile but nods, satisfied. She takes a step forward and her fingers probe to the next pair of ribs.

"What does Georgia do?" Danielle whispers.

"She's a personal assistant," Phoebe says.

"How do you get promoted if you're a personal assistant?"

Phoebe shrugs. Allie shushes them again.

"Sixth true pair. Romance, sexual energy, partnership. Surface: largely smooth, one pronounced notch mid-body on the right rib, which is common. It signifies the one that got away. Costal cartilage starts early with wavy seams. Short-bodied ribs. Not the luckiest in love, I take it?" Here she does raise an eyebrow in the direction of the window. Danielle glances at Allie and Phoebe for confirmation. They're both snickering. "But the costal grooves are hungry. My finger tucks right in there, snug as a bug. She'll find someone and she won't let go."

"Sounds codependent," says Danielle. Allie gives a quick nod. Phoebe tilts her head, perhaps offended, and Danielle grins.

The Ospex takes a moment to get to the next rib, as if she has to establish some sort of grip, though it's just those two fingers sliding under Georgia's skin. Danielle imagines they have to settle on the bone in just the right way before they can skate cleanly. Blood freckles the Ospex's arms and the team moves in with suction often. The Ospex talks with her eyes closed. The reading has to move quickly to minimize the risk of infection. Danielle finds the sterilization team bristling off to the left, waiting to be let loose when the Ospex finishes.

"Seventh true pair. Social connections, empathy, popularity. Oh." The Ospex's brow wrinkles. "Asymmetry here, more than before. Left rib is smooth, right one considerably more pocked."

Two-faced, Danielle thinks, triumphant.

"Complex character: She's that rare mix of introvert and extrovert. Great at parties, but only if she wants to be there. Otherwise she sulks."

Phoebe laughs at that. Danielle inspects Allie's

face, wondering how it will shift, how it will show a terrible but necessary realization. She doesn't expect Allie to purge them from her life immediately, but she thinks they'll fade out, fall into the lower-priority spaces that have been sitting, reserved.

Oh my, this one enjoys drama, she pictures the Ospex saying, those middle fingers skittering roughly inside her own chest.

But it's not just that, Danielle thinks. It's that Allie deserves better. She has to hear it from someone else. She has to.

"She keeps her secrets," the Ospex says. "Not an easy person to get to know. She will have but a few close confidantes all her life, and it won't be an easy job for them." And then her fingers slide lower, pushing the skin into that traveling hill, and she's on to the final rib in the reading.

But that can't be right. The seventh pair is the crucial one, the one for friendships. She's left so much out.

"First false pair—"

"Wait," Danielle says. "That was nothing. Did she cut it short?"

"—fears, the subconscious—"

"What do you mean it's nothing?" Phoebe says. "She didn't really talk about her!"

"—sharp angle, greedy for the seventh rib's cartilage—"

"Calm down," Allie says, and Danielle sees her constricted, gasping at the center of this awful knot.

"But—"

"—loneliness—"

"Wait, what were you expecting?" Phoebe asks.

"I don't know, maybe something about how you two almost killed her?"

"—the ocean—"

"Excuse me?"

"Both of you, be quiet!"

"—being forgotten."

The Ospex takes a visible breath and slides her fingers out of Georgia. "Thank you," she says. The sterilization team rushes in, elbows working like pistons.

The receptionist needs to fetch the next candidate, but she reenters the room too early. They're yelling at one another.

"What the fuck are you even saying, though? Are you talking about something you actually know nothing about? Something that didn't involve you at all? Are you really doing that now? Today?" Phoebe stands in front of Danielle's chair, blocking her view into the reading room.

Danielle's posture is straight, defiant. She looks like she might launch herself at Phoebe's throat.

"Don't fucking bully me," she says.

"All right, if this day is supposed to be about me, can we stop?" Allie kneads her temples with her fingers. "One of us has to go next."

"Allie, come on. The reading didn't say anything about what they did to you." Danielle sweeps her hand up and down, scanning the length of Allie's body. "We should get our money back."

Allie doesn't answer. She clutches at her knees.

The receptionist knows she isn't qualified to mediate, but she can't leave now. She's awed by the purity of anger on display. One reading in, and they've all let go. It's such a stark sign of progress, an obvious dam breaking, that she has the urge to applaud. But she keeps her palms flat on the wall behind her and waits.

"Danielle should go next," Phoebe says.

"I'm sorry, what?"

"You're instigating shit, so I think you should go next. It's getting toxic in here."

Danielle twists her body in the chair so that all of her is facing Allie.

"Allie," she says, "I would never have done something like that to you. They're not your friends."

The receptionist realizes in a moment of panic that if they don't resolve this soon, she will indeed have to take action. There's another group reading scheduled for 3:00 p.m. She looks to Allie, apologetic, joining the other two women in a silent request for a ruling. From the direction of the reading room, she hears the familiar sounds of water running hard, gloves snapping, tools chattering against one another as a new set is laid out. She lists them in her head, imagines her own voice calling for them, strong and sure: dilators, clamps, scalpels, calipers—

"I also think you should go next," Allie says, taking Danielle's hand. Danielle starts to cry.

"Thank you," says Phoebe.

"It's so I can talk to Phoebe," Allie says. "Please. Do it for me. I promise it'll be okay."

The receptionist sees her opening. She steps forward, puts her hand in the crook of Danielle's elbow, eases her up, the same way she's seen the Ospex do it.

"Come on, dear," she says. She's firm and professional.

Danielle starts to move with her. She sniffles as they walk to the prep room, but she doesn't protest.

"She's right, you know," the receptionist says. "And after this, I'm sure you'll all be able to communicate better. I know it can be hard when you don't hear what you expect."

The receptionist is grateful that they're all doing the standard package, the four ribs that are easiest to reach. People who get the whole cage read—all the way up to the first pair, all the way back to the tubercles, all the way down through the floaters—have to recover at the clinic overnight. She wouldn't want to wait on these four in the morning. They'd yell at her about the pain-med dosages and the fact that the beds aren't adjustable.

When she gets a reading herself, recovery will be a cinch. She knows all the recommended postures and the symptoms of infection to watch for. The hardest part will be trying not to laugh too much, which apparently hurts more than anything else.

After a few weeks, though, she'll have the twin scars to show off. Anyone who looks at her when she's naked, or even just in a bathing suit, will know she's been truly seen.

Every time she spoke with Allie in the months after the accident, the apologies sucked the honesty out of Phoebe, leaving her drained. Georgia was different—she coated herself in guilt, let it harden into a seal. She apologized, cried, apologized for crying, apologized for "making it about her," apologized if she was even two minutes late to practice Allie's physical therapy drills with her. Phoebe had been alone, abandoned in the realm of nuanced thought.

Phoebe did ask Georgia, once, whose fault it had been. Whose fault it had been, *really*. Who had been the gullible one who fell for such an obvious prank. Georgia had squinted at her like she was an alien.

It's all ancient history now, and Phoebe had not wanted to turn that earth.

"She had no right to talk to me like that. She doesn't know anything."

"Danielle's my friend too. I want you all to get along this week, and at the wedding. Can we put it behind us, please?" Allie's voice cracks, maybe under the irony of her demand. She's marrying the same surgeon that caught the muscle wasting in her fractured leg. She plans on seeing the same face that had hovered over her in a mask, the face associated with the worst of her pain, every day. She's mummifying her damage in him, and her judgment too. Every time they're together, he appraises Phoebe and Georgia with an infuriating patience that cleaves the ground between them: him and Allie on one side, forever-children on the other. Of course, he and Danielle get along.

"She hasn't put it behind her and she wasn't even there," Phoebe says. "You know, she literally seems jealous that she wasn't involved."

"She thinks she has to fight for me. That's her thing." Allie sounds charmed, under a spell. All this serves to make Danielle look saintly when she's wheeled in, like a downed martyr attended by acolytes.

You'll be in there soon, Phoebe thinks. She'll read you next.

And find what? The Ospex is clearly a charlatan. Nothing she says is specific or damning. As the woman slots her fingers into Danielle, Phoebe listens for the sound of it happening, imagines it's the noise made by putting on a soaking wet slipper. She puts her hands on her own rib cage to follow along, though it makes her feel slightly ill.

"Fifth true pair. Surface: a little scratched, but largely smooth. The costal grooves are canted, favoring the bottom of the body, which denotes an inclination for travel as part of business."

"Does she travel for consulting?" Phoebe asks. Allie nods.

"Huh, lucky guess."

"You don't... believe?" Allie asks.

"I don't know? I'm trying to be open-minded."

"Why would you come to this if you don't even believe in it?"

"Because it's your bachelorette party! Of course I'm going to come!"

"—client-facing. She's career-oriented too, she'll stay in the same field. Straight as an arrow."

Phoebe thinks Danielle is a more profuse bleeder than Georgia, and this strikes her as appropriate. The Ospex slides her fingers to the next rib and a red bubble gluts out. The team suctions more frequently.

"Sixth true pair. Goodness, I'm getting... almost perfect symmetry. She knows what she wants. A true romantic. Cartilage seams are also neat. Medium-bodied ribs, I call them Goldilocks bones: not too long and not too short. Some might think her tastes are a little white-bread, but she'll be happy, and that's what matters. She shouldn't compromise."

Danielle's reading is as vague as Georgia's. Allie makes affirmative humming noises after every statement. Phoebe becomes more and more nauseated as she focuses on the cuts, transposes them onto her own body.

Stop it, she thinks. You'll be knocked out. Dead to the world.

But why is she even here? Would Allie really do this to get at the nonexistent heart of a hoax gone wrong? A hoax that no fifteen-year-old should have believed in the first place?

"Do you still think about the accident a lot, Al?"

The Ospex is saying that Danielle is unfalteringly loyal, trusting to a fault.

"What do you mean, do I think about it? Of course I think about it, sometimes."

"A lot? Are you, like, *haunted*? Do you think we were—"

"Oh my god, I'm not going to reassure you right now, Phoebe. I want to watch this."

The Ospex moves to the last rib, the false one. She begins to detail Danielle's fear of heights and public speaking.

Phoebe hears the blood circulating beneath her skin in a perfect, unbroken system, begging to go undisturbed.

"Did you book the readings because of the accident?" she asks. "Do you still not trust us?"

"Shut up, Phoebe."

"Is this some eye-for-an-eye bullshit? We have to go on the operating table, too, because you did?"

"It's been more than ten years. Get over yourself."

Phoebe looks away from the window as they begin to stitch Danielle shut. She flips through memories of phone calls, updates on college, on boys, on personal philosophies. She had called Allie after her most painful breakup, sobbed at her—bared enough. She and Georgia had done a thoughtless thing, but Allie had always had agency and more than half a brain. To say otherwise, to blame only them, diminishes her.

The receptionist opens the door and Phoebe jumps in her seat.

"Shall we?" the receptionist says, extending her hand.

"Go on," says Allie. "I want to hear what she says."

"What do you think you're going to learn that you don't already know?" Phoebe asks. The receptionist is trying to lift her by the elbow. Phoebe shakes her off, stands up on her own. She can't think of a way out. She lingers, stepping slowly behind the receptionist, and turns back to Allie just before she gets to the door.

"I didn't push it," she says, desperate, lying. "I felt it move on the board, just like you."

"What?" Allie stands up.

"It wasn't me. It was all Georgia."

Allie sighs. Her shoulders lower and her lips pull into a thin line.

"Let's just see what she says."

The receptionist catches the last bit of Phoebe's reading.

"Confrontational," the Ospex says. "The rough cartilage seams mean she loves a debate but can take it too far."

Sounds about right, the receptionist thinks.

She goes to help Allie up, to support her while she walks, if need be, but Allie waves her away.

"I'm not doing it," she says.

The receptionist rarely encounters cold feet once the deposit is down. She gives Allie time to elaborate, but nothing passes between them.

Sad, she thinks. It's her party, and she's the quietest of the four. She wonders if she mistook shyness for frostiness, back when they all signed their forms. She wishes Allie still wanted her reading, so she could find out.

"I'm sorry, but I can't get you the deposit back," she says.

"That's okay. Can I please see my friends?"

The recovery room is dim, the steady beeping of the monitors the only noise. Georgia, Danielle, and Phoebe are uneven hills under light blue sheets.

"They'll wake up in the order they were read," the receptionist says. "Should be about an hour. And there's an aftercare demonstration for the incisions, but it's nothing elaborate. Want me to give you a preview?"

"No, thank you."

"Can I get you anything? A glass of water?"

"No. I'd just like to be here when they come out of it."

The receptionist nods. She's reluctant to leave Allie alone, but there's nothing left for her to ask, and she knows she's being selfish—she hates to abandon a mystery. But some people, she tells herself, aren't ready to be seen, and you have to respect their choices.

* * *

Does she know them better now? Certainly she should.

Allie will tell them, when they wake up, that the Ospex declined to read her due to her medical history, the possibility of aggravating past traumas. Her fiancé will pick them up in the evening, and they'll be ferried to a calming, sterile hotel room. The next night, they can watch the readings on her laptop. They'll get room service for every meal.

She flexes her fingers, strokes the sheets on someone's bed. In the low light, and in sleep, their faces have softened into formlessness. Each time she tries to pinpoint a feature, she finds it could belong to any of the three. None of them move beyond the small shiftings of breath.

What has she learned?

She remembers their fingers on the planchette, the candlelight that shone on their cheeks. She remembers it moving, remembers the stitch in her throat, how her mouth dried up when the thing actually worked, actually started to spell.

A-L-L-I-E-G-A-T-O-R

"It's my dad!" she had shrieked. "Don't take your hands off, it's my dad!" Their fingers thrumming, the planchette scraping to the next letter, the next letter. She had felt the connection all the way up her arms, shaking in her shoulders.

Whose bed is this?

There's a sound like someone picking their fingernails, and she realizes that it's her, only she's picking at someone's dissolvable stitches. It's an unobtrusive sound, even when the stitches snap. Allie's had not been dissolvable. They had needed forceps to hold and twist and unwind them from her.

She'd tried to know them in so many ways, to understand who they were and what they'd done, what they might be capable of doing. Even Danielle, who hadn't been there—there was something hard about her, the potential for cruelty, a steady sharpening of a hidden knife. How could she believe anything they said? She couldn't generate enough trust from the substance of herself. She had needed to see inside them.

It doesn't matter whose bed this is. One end of the cut purses, like lips letting out a small sigh. The skin wanted releasing. Allie's finger coasts along the opening, a planchette hovering over a board, ready for a letter. There's the promise of a hard surface underneath. No one else's fingers are here to muddle the spelling. But when she slips inside, finds the bone, slides her fingers along the surface, it's smooth and blank.

AN AUDACIOUS MAN

by EVAN JAMES

THERE ONCE WAS A gay couple in their thirties who wanted to have children, or anyway it was the subject of a certain amount of conflicted conversation. "Either a little daughter or a dog," said one.

"You mean it's the same to you?" his partner said.

"I just want to be something's daddy."

"Neither is just a *thing*, Harry."

Harry was a known shit-starter, so his partner, Phil, couldn't be sure what to make of this exchange.

In the early days of their courtship, Phil had said he didn't want children. Later, he revised his opinion to say he might consider it "with the right person," that he was "open to being surprised by life." ("Are you saying the 'right person' might not be *me*?" Harry had countered. "Do I not surprise you?") All Phil could be certain of now, and of that just barely, was that he could not trust his own apparent convictions and desires—always so vehement in the moment—not to change over time. His moods waxed and waned as regularly as the moon itself.

"The moon itself," he whispered in bed one evening.

"Huh?" said Harry. "The moon?"

"I don't know, Hare. When I think about having a child, I also think about all the orphaned children wandering this horrible earth."

"You think Genghis Khan ever thought about that?" asked Harry, almost slurring his words.

"Here we go."

Harry shrugged. "Genghis Khan was somebody who fully embraced the violent, creative urges of the life force. He's probably a shared ancestor of ours too. We should honor and respect him. Hell, it wouldn't hurt to think more like him while we're at it."

Phil sighed. "I guess we're talking about Genghis Khan now."

"Why not?" asked Harry.

"I can think of a couple million reasons. Didn't he kill a lot of people?"

"He did what he had to do, Phillip. He was an audacious man. He united the nomads. You think that was easy for him?"

Phil could see that his partner meant to wear him down with this nonsense. Harry had made it one of his missions in life to help Phil grow a thicker skin—he thought he was overly sensitive. To live life to the fullest, Harry felt—and said, often—one must take *bold risks*.

Around this time, a serendipity: a lesbian couple they were close to and sometimes had dinner parties with announced their own shared desire to have a child. They, too, were in conflict about how to go about it: one thought it was selfish to have a child through traditional conception, the other thought it was important to be selfish sometimes; one thought such exceptions were in flagrant contradiction to all other values they held dear, the other felt strongly that visceral immersion in human experience was the ultimate value, the one that trumped everything else, and that all other values and convictions must continually be reconsidered and reshaped around it.

"So you're saying it's less human to adopt?" asked one of the women.

At this, her partner started crying. Mind you, they were over for dinner at Harry and Phil's.

"Here's an idea," offered Harry. "What if we all shared one baby? That would solve everything, right?"

Phil gave him a look. Now was not the time for one of his pranks.

"I'm serious," complained Harry.

"But I want my *own* baby!" cried the woman who had just reduced her partner to tears. This was an appreciable risk, and it paid off: everyone laughed.

After that evening, they all retreated into themselves for a think. Harry started a group email chain that week. Every few days he would provoke them with famous quotes about the power of action, to seed their minds:

Courage is the commitment to begin without any guarantee of success.

—Johann Wolfgang von Goethe

Do you want to know who you are? Don't ask. Act! Action will delineate and define you.

—Thomas Jefferson

Take the first step in faith. You don't have to see the whole staircase, just take the first step.

—Dr. Martin Luther King Jr.

A week later, he sent them a manifesto declaring that, all through human history, that which stood the test of time was predicated on some act of audacity. He titled this manifesto "The Theater of Audacity"; he went on to propose that rather than splitting one child and heir between the four of them, they redouble their commitment to audacity—inherent already, he claimed, in their "decadent homosexual lifestyles"—by piercing the last frontier of sexuality and respectability and dedicating themselves to "heterohomosexuality." Partner swapping, in effect: becoming married dyads composed of a gay man and a lesbian who had monogamous sex with each other, and who married and had children.

"I got your email," said Phil. "What you are proposing is ridiculous, and it hurt my feelings."

"That's what they told Copernicus," said Harry. "Newton too."

"That doesn't make sense," said Phil, but Harry had already pulled out his phone to email another quote.

The thing is, Harry really meant what he said, and he was determined to put his Theater of Audacity into practice. And because his partner and friends rejected his idea as a preposterous farce, he began distancing himself from them, sending quotes about the wages of fear:

> *We can easily forgive a child who is afraid of the dark;*
> *the real tragedy of life is when men are afraid of the light.*
>
> —Plato

> *The brave man is not he who does not feel afraid, but he who conquers that fear.*
>
> —Nelson Mandela

You have to decide who you are and force the world to deal with you, not with its idea of you.

—James Baldwin

"All men, of course," muttered one-half of the lesbian couple. But it made no difference: Harry had grown tired of what he perceived as their cowardice and his own; he was determined, it seemed, to make a bold and "generative" move; he felt that if he didn't do so, he would deprive his one and only life of some significant meaning it would otherwise never have.

Harry became more and more distant, more mysterious, even cryptic. He left his partner; he replied to emails with densely theoretical polemics on the importance of bold and audacious action. Most bewilderingly, after vanishing for a few years, he began to appear around town with a woman, one known to be a lifelong lesbian, whom he introduced to others as his wife. The two of them wore uniforms of rainbow Pride garb, engaged in enthusiastic public displays of affection, and were always dragging two children around with them. Neither would answer questions about whether the children had been conceived by them or adopted, borrowed or stolen. It goes without saying that people gossiped and rumor-mongered, feared for the fate of these children, even though, to the innocent eye, they were not so unusual looking as far as families go. And that is how they came to achieve local fame in the manner of one of those curious individuals or couples that roam the city, whose secrets charge the air around them but are never, or almost never, revealed in their entirety.

THE REANIMATOR

by MIKKEL ROSENGAARD

I'D NEVER BELIEVED IN an afterlife. You know
my type: rational, unsentimental—but then Bjarke
Johannesen returned from the dead.

It had been four weeks since the funeral when
he came back to find me scrolling my phone at
two in the morning. My doctor had warned me,
"No social media before bed," but let's be honest:
There are plenty of things stronger than my will.
The Shiba-headed dust cloud. Awkward monkey
puppet. Woman screaming at cat with broccoli.

The night Bjarke returned, I had been sharing a meme of a skeleton doing the laundry: "When you're dead inside but highly functional."

I was thirty-one, my girlfriend had left me for a younger man, and I had recently witnessed my best friend succumbing to a slow and gruesome death, so I felt I could relate. Scrolling the memes of confused animals and desperate people made me feel less alone, though they no longer made me laugh. The same absurdity wasn't funny after the hundredth time. And most nights I scrolled more than a hundred memes, all dank, all plucked from the rubber-duck pond of anxiety with a blinking plastic pole.

Beyond the memes were the comment threads. I was looking for what I couldn't find in my job as a freelance copywriter: namely, the throb of community. When Bjarke's icon slid into my DMs, I was commenting on an opossum guarding a pile of trash: "me when my mom asks what i'm doing with my life lmao." A circle haloed Bjarke's face, spiraling in the grapefruit pastels of early dawn. I barely thought about it—I just clicked it out of habit. A flash of white, then I was presented with

Bjarke Johannesen's unshaven mug, lips stretched in one of his sloth-like smiles. Behind him was an aisle of waffle mix, hundreds of identical yellow boxes. He started talking.

"I just wanted to say—I know we didn't really get to say goodbye. But I just want you to know, I feel really lucky. I got to leave before things got dark." The camera shook, and then came the unmistakable laughter of my best friend, or former best friend, relaxed as ever, almost sleepy-sounding.

"When I left, bro, I was in love," he went on. "Like, surrounded by love. I got lucky, and I feel bad for you all. Now you have to go through this whole mess. But I trust you guys. The world just wants us to be happy. You'll be fine."

He smiled at me, without irony this time, a peaceful smile—mindless, even. Then the video was over.

I fumbled to restart the clip, but it was one of those ghostly messages that evaporate after thirty seconds. For a moment I cursed myself for not taking a screenshot, like any intelligent person would have done. I stood up to grab my phone. I felt like telling someone. I felt like crying. I felt like laughing in disbelief—but it was two in the morning, my roommates were asleep, and it's not like I had any friends I could call that late. So after spending half an hour scrolling the comments on Bjarke's account and not finding anything but polite messages from bereaved friends and former coworkers, I went to the bathroom and brushed my teeth.

As I said, I am not an unreasonable man. Cowardly, spineless, maybe—but not unreasonable. I didn't really believe it was my best friend coming back from the grave to say goodbye online. So who was it? It was clearly Bjarke's face and voice, and Bjarke was clearly dead. I had spent two weeks by his deathbed, distractedly watching the Tour de France as I held his hand, doing my best to laugh at his fiancée, Nanna's, jokes, now and then catching a flash of white terror in his eyes, a look I had never seen on anyone and hope I'll never have to see again. I'd even seen his corpse, appearing all waxen on the narrow trolley in the hospital chapel. His beard had seemed fake and his sisters were fighting: the older one telling Nanna to stop taking photos, and the younger one telling the older one to mind her own business. And then Bjarke's mother threw herself over the trolley, sort of tugging at his legs, crying, "My boy, my little boy," over and over until an orderly had the decency to corral us into the courtyard, like a flock of confused cattle, and that's the last time I'd seen Bjarke or his body.

How cruel of us, I thought, brushing my teeth at two in the morning. How callous, abandoning his poor body in that hospital dungeon, on that bizarrely narrow trolley. Why had we left him there? With no wake, no lamentation, no cutting of the fingernails—with nothing but the stale bureaucracy of dying. Maybe that was why Bjarke had returned, I thought, chewing on my toothbrush. Because we abandoned him. What a petty fate that seemed, haunting the platforms for all eternity. For a moment I was afraid that I, too, might end up with nothing better to haunt—no family attic, no mansion staircase, not even an ex-wife's laundry room—and I would have to spend my afterlife lost in the electromagnetic currents or whatever it was that had beamed Bjarke through the wind and the rain and the backyard trampolines encircling Copenhagen.

But then I came to my senses—it was only a video. Like anyone who'd spent any time online that year, I had seen the only known photograph of Billy the Kid turned into a live video by AI. Well, I thought, that's what they had done to poor Bjarke. The software was impressive, you had to admit—no glitches, hardly pixelated at all—but the pristine video quality notwithstanding, I found it crude and in bad taste.

Still, as I lay in bed, I couldn't fall asleep. My reactions were confusing. I felt elated for having been visited by Bjarke, grateful for having heard his voice, and surprised to hear that he felt lucky, but also annoyed at my own gullibility, disgusted by my relapse into superstition. And I felt a growing sense of outrage: Who had such nerve? For once, I didn't feel dead inside. That's what a decade of scrolling my phone had taught me: amid the advice ducks and chemtrail news, the internet can still summon something raw that we Westerners need but are afraid to face head-on. But that night in bed, checking Bjarke's account one last time, I didn't think about all that. I just wanted to know who had reanimated Bjarke.

The next morning at my desk I searched for "dead friend on social media." I poked around the subforums /DeepFakes and /MachineLearning. I even sent a few emails to the interactive designers who had reanimated Billy the Kid, but those grad school grave robbers couldn't tell me anything I didn't already know about my friend. I couldn't stop staring at the little icons in my DMs, hoping against all sense that Bjarke's face would reappear, haloed in grapefruit pastels. Had I been hallucinating? Or had I really experienced an encounter, some glitch in the universe—the husband dies and the lights start flickering. A mother has a heart attack, the son hears her voice from the cupboard, and the dog starts freaking out.

For the rest of the week, Bjarke didn't show up again in my DMs. None of our common friends had been visited by his account, save for Jeppe, who, when I pressed him on the subject, admitted to having seen a similar apparition. This disturbed me. Why were they targeting Jeppe and me? Was it some scam, a twisted update to the Nigerian email? Or a morbid new advertisement trick based on our search histories?

"And why is he in the baking aisle?" I asked
Jeppe. "He never baked a thing in his life."

We were sitting in Jeppe's condo, drinking at
the marble kitchen counter. Like me, Jeppe had
met Bjarke at university. But unlike me and Bjarke,
Jeppe never posted memes, didn't play video games,
and had a demanding publicity job for the Social
Democrats in Parliament.

"It's probably a troll account," Jeppe said,
showing me his overflowing DMs. "They are always
trolling us at work."

"Who are?" I reminded him that I had left
Bjarke's deathbed to deal with an overdue freelance
job. By the time I filed the copy for those pepperoni
dog treats, two days later, Bjarke was in a coma. "And
how do they know I didn't get to say goodbye?"

Jeppe gave an impatient shrug. "Ah, it's better
to forget about that stuff," he said, deleting the
DMs with three elegant swipes. "That's my policy.
Forget, forget, forget."

I spent Sunday morning sharing memes, commenting on videos, and hearting women in yoga pants.

Every so often I went to Bjarke's account, looked around for the grapefruit halo, and was relieved not to find it. I was ready to follow Jeppe's advice, forget the whole thing, and get on with my life—but just as I was settling into the warm ball pit of internet hysteria, a flash of red caught my eye. A small crimson flag notified me that Nanna Vest had tagged me in a post.

In the photo, Bjarke, Nanna, and I were sprawled out on a beach blanket, laughing at the camera. There were other photos in the post—Bjarke eating a hot dog, Bjarke and Nanna with matching propeller hats—which commemorated the fact that it had been one month since he passed away. "I miss him more than I can describe," Nanna had written below the photo, next to a broken red heart. "I always thought we'd have more time."

I didn't know why she had tagged me—it was the first time I'd heard from her since the funeral. For a few moments, as I opened Nanna's account and began scrolling her posts, I experienced a kind of vertigo, a glance into the bottomless pit of longing. Her account was mostly pictures of Bjarke, peppered with wedding photos and snapshots of graphic novels and garishly decorated pastries. She worked as a graphic designer at an ad agency; judging from the campaign videos she was tagged in, she seemed to be skilled at her job. I clicked on her highlighted posts, which I discovered were a timeline of her relationship with Bjarke. Their photos surprised me. I would never have imagined that Bjarke took so many couple selfies. I clicked through the photos for what seemed like a long time, hearting most of them, trying to come up with a way to ask Nanna if she had been visited by Bjarke, without sounding like I'd lost my mind.

It was early in the evening when I blundered into her DMs. "This might sound weird, but have you heard anything from Bjarke's account?"

Nanna read my message right away, and I watched the three blue dots dancing in our thread, indicating that she was typing a reply. Then the dots disappeared, and the green circle under her icon faded. I worried I had upset her, triggered her grief with my graceless question, but soon the snaking dots were back again, followed by another log-off. It continued like that for fifteen minutes: Nanna typing and deleting, and me watching the little conga line of dots dancing in the corner of my screen, trying to think through the fog of guilt about who was trolling us, if it was indeed a troll account, which no longer seemed obvious to me.

"Hope you are doing okay," I finally wrote, adding a conciliatory smiling cat face. "Let me know if there is anything I can do to help."

This time her reply came through immediately. "Can you come over?"

I wasn't sure what she meant, so I kept quiet and watched the dots.

"Right now?"

I told her I had a deadline, but that I'd stop by after I'd polished the copy for the banana-themed shirts. By the time I pressed the buzzer of her apartment, the last daylight was fading from the gray, low-hanging, office-tiled sky. Nanna was still living in the apartment she had shared with Bjarke, on a quiet street behind the lakes. Through the window I could see people moving up there, more than one, and then the door buzzed open. When I arrived on the third floor, a shorter, middle-aged version of Nanna was peeking out from behind the door— Nanna's mother, I presumed. The woman stepped back, to make space, I thought, but when I entered the apartment she continued backing down the hallway.

"She's in the bedroom," she called out.

As I untied my shoes, I noticed Nanna's brother in the living room, plates and cups on the table, and I felt as if I were interrupting some low-key family gathering. Nanna's mother backed into the living room with a little cough and repeated that Nanna was in the bedroom, waiting for me. I knocked, waited a few seconds, and when nothing happened, I entered.

The bedroom was cool and dim. The blinds were drawn, and the only source of light was a violet glow emanating from a laptop. Nanna was sitting on the bed, lit by the screen. She seemed different from when I'd seen her at the funeral. She wore a pigeon-blue top and a long, low-rise skirt that made her resemble the meme-able skeletons I had been sharing at a breakneck clip—all ribs and clavicles and hip bones. The Nanna I knew had a round face and full cheeks and was chronically on futile diets. No carbs, no sugar, only mashed peas, only butter in the coffee. Not that she ever needed it—she had always seemed young, normal, healthy. But the Nanna in front of me looked terrorized, like bulimia missing a flight at the airport. As we spoke, she tied her hair into a braid with the shaky fingers of a feeble pensioner, though her firm gaze still indicated a woman of resolve, someone who knew exactly what she wanted. When I asked whether she had lost weight, she rolled her eyes.

"The irony of grief," she said. "I've never felt worse and never looked better."

"Why are you in the bedroom?"

I didn't realize it at the time, but from that moment, everything in my life began to change. Nanna reached across the nightstand and picked up a hair band. As she nervously finished her braid, I mentioned that Jeppe and I had been visited by Bjarke, or by his troll account. This seemed to make an impression on her, for she asked several times about Jeppe's reaction, and whether we had contacted the platform. I told her we hadn't.

"God, Bjarke's account," she said, coaxing those emaciated cheeks of hers into a smile. "God knows I've seen plenty of Bjarke's account."

She said it flatly, with a voice full of sarcasm. Then she reached for the computer and asked if she could show me something. There was something she'd been meaning to tell me, something rather complicated—if I didn't mind?

"Not at all," I said. She gestured toward the bed; I sat down next to her. Nanna logged on to the subforum /GriefSupport, and as she clicked in and out of the posts, quickly scrolling through the threads, she began telling me about the difficult days after the funeral.

"You know, when someone dies, how you can't get access to their account?" she asked.

Well, that policy had driven her to the brink of madness. She was convinced there were more photos of Bjarke on his account—and if she didn't get hold of them, they would be lost forever. She had spent hours answering the labyrinthine queries of the chatbots, typing out long emails to the legal department, threatening litigation. She became obsessed with the thought of Bjarke's photos—locked away forever, stolen by the platform—and once, on a call, she had even offered a customer support agent in Hyderabad a hefty bribe, but of course he hadn't had the tools to help her.

"Because it's difficult to hack an account," Nanna told me. "But it's a lot easier to get someone else to hack it for you."

Nanna took out her phone, showed me a Russian chat app, and told me about a cousin of hers, a cyber-security contractor, and his co-hackers in the defense industry. I should have picked up on where she was going with this, but I've always been slow-witted. I just nodded and waited for her to continue.

"Of course," she said, "those elite hackers don't waste their time breaking into regular accounts."

They have hired help for that. In Florianópolis. In former Soviet republics. The accounts of the dead are the easiest to hack, the users on the Russian chat app told her. The dead don't react to alerts about suspicious account activity. The dead don't alert support. Dictionary attacks, they call it in the business. Rainbow tables. Here Nanna paused, keeping her large eyes fixed on me. And in that moment I had a flash of inspiration, like in a game of *Jeopardy!*: first the answer, then the question.

Who missed Bjarke enough to reanimate him?

"So I wired the money to Brazil," Nanna said, and a few days later she received the password to

Bjarke's account. With extreme care, she spent a week cataloging the pictures of Bjarke, archiving them, even animating some of them with AI. And once she was done, once there were no more photos or videos to archive, she felt a void opening. She couldn't eat. She couldn't sleep. She couldn't work, and was given a medical leave of absence, but the long days alone in the apartment only made it worse. She felt she was regressing to some infant state, spending her days in bed, nourished on oatmeal, napping and crying softly. Her family started coming over—her parents and brother taking turns keeping a vigil by her side.

As she spoke, I tried to read Nanna's face, which looked odd in the glow of the laptop, as if scrolling the subforum had made her blush. I also thought I could hear her voice trembling. People in grief do many strange things, she told me. The only animal that commits suicide. The only animal that starves itself. That cuts lines into its skin, that reports to the subforum /GriefSupport and scrolls through the stories: overdoses, cancer, cardiac arrest. She spent whole nights on that subforum, stalking the accounts of the grief-stricken. Nanna placed the laptop in front of me, showing me a post titled "I feel like the worst husband in the world."

Here she glanced up, timid, or maybe bashful. Through the wall, I could hear her mother and brother clearing the dishes in the kitchen. She went on.

One night, Nanna had read about a young dad who had lost his wife. It had all happened so quickly—he was picking up their kid when the doctors had to intubate her. She never woke up again, he never got to say goodbye, and the fact that she never visited him in a dream made him feel worse. After Nanna finished reading the young dad's post, she had felt a renewed resolve. She had wired money to Florianópolis. And when the password arrived, Nanna animated a video of the dead wife, and logged on to the account.

Nanna was sitting cross-legged on the bed, still fiddling with her braid. By this point, I had realized who was behind Bjarke's apparition, and I was shocked and confused. It was easy enough to imagine what Nanna would be doing with Bjarke's animation—or at least it was to me, having enjoyed countless POV instruction videos myself—but sending unsolicited ghost clips to strangers seemed like a disturbing, even dangerous hobby. I would have liked to tell her she should be ashamed, but somehow I couldn't. I was staring into her face, her eyes as big as those of Japanese manga characters, but with an unbending look in them, the gaze of a zealot, I thought, a vigilante gestalt therapist.

"How did he react?" I asked. "The young dad."

Nanna closed her eyes. I tried to see if she was about to cry, but all I could read on her face was a hint of exhaustion. After the dead wife, she told me, she had reanimated dozens of accounts—dead people she found on the subforum /GriefSupport. A mother returned from an overdose to say goodbye to her son. A daughter reappeared on her birthday, asking her dad to pet the cat. No one ever complained to the platform. No one mentioned anything on /GriefSupport. And who would believe them if they did? Life went on, but their sorrow wasn't the same. People began sending messages to the dead accounts. "I could feel you today at the exam." "Was it you last night who scared that man away?" People started crying when they saw a pigeon peering in from the windowsill. They had experienced something they couldn't explain, something like closure, she thought at first, and then it seemed like grace, which made her own life meaningful.

Nanna wiped tears from her eyes. As she reached for the box of tissues on the nightstand, I was filled with the same confusion I'd felt after I first encountered Bjarke's ghost. I felt disturbed and shocked, but also grateful that she'd tried to relieve my guilt, and impressed that this was how she was coping with her loss, like a Robin Hood of grief, robbing from the dead and giving to the living. Me, I was coping with memes and porn and video games.

"But why the baking aisle?" I asked, suddenly remembering the supermarket setting of the video.

"Oh, that was just stock video from a campaign we did. It was easy to paste Bjarke in there."

"And why Jeppe and me—why not his other friends?"

Nanna looked down at her nails, and almost simultaneously a blush spread across her cheeks. "I don't know. I like you two the best."

I was worried I had upset her, or that she would start crying again, although on closer inspection she didn't seem all that troubled. From behind the door, I heard the voices of Nanna's brother and mother and a crinkling of raincoats. Then the door to the apartment slammed, and I heard their voices echoing from the staircase. We were alone in the apartment, sitting in the dim bedroom, on opposite ends of the bed.

Blowing her nose, Nanna sat up straight and asked me to forgive her for what she had done with Bjarke.

"Don't worry about it," I said. "I enjoyed seeing him."

"You must think I'm a total freak," Nanna said.

I assured her I had done freakier things online and that she didn't have to apologize. But she went on anyway, giving me an apology that was more like an account of how she'd ended up here. It was a strange feeling, sitting on Bjarke's bed, listening to her speaking. For a moment I imagined the disapproving ghost of Bjarke looking down at us and felt a surge of shame. But soon enough that pang of superstition faded.

We must have talked for five or six hours that night. Maybe more. She told me of her parents' divorce, her brother's mental illness, her mother's sandwich shop in Hvidovre, her relationships with boyfriends and her brief stint as a lesbian, her hopes of writing graphic novels and the burning self-hate that sent all creative endeavors up in flames, and how Bjarke had rescued her from all that, how handsome he was, and how comfortable in his skin, so self-confidently lazy that everyone felt relaxed, at ease, unthreatened in his company. She told me of the terrible names she wanted to be called, which she had never dared to tell anyone but him, and of their dreams of starting a family—two girls and a boy—a dream she compared to inserting a pacemaker in a lime-scaled heart. And as I listened, I discovered a new sensation, a whole subforum of memories and feelings I had suddenly gained access to, and I told her of my numb childhood; my string of failed relationships; the intensely dramatic women I found myself attracted to, my longing to take care of them, which was maybe just a foil to hide my dread that no one would ever take care of me, and the twisted things I secretly wanted to do to them, reducing my lovers to a state of drooling dependency; my chronic restlessness; my inability to hold down a job; and how Bjarke had been the one calm constant in my muddled life, someone to guide me, someone I hoped would one day show me how to love a woman and a child; on and on, until the first blackbird started singing from the street, and we both fell silent.

At this point Bjarke and Nanna's bedroom had become blue and oceanic, the indigo dawn seeping in through the blinds and shadows pouring out from under the furniture. Then Nanna asked, with some abruptness, what I was going to do. "Nothing," I told her, and promised that her secret was safe with me. "Don't worry," I said. "I won't tell Jeppe." She thanked me but added that she didn't care what other people thought. She was beyond all that now.

I watched as she untangled her braid. I felt calm, at peace with what was about to happen, and I think she felt the same. After a while, I said, "I should probably go." She gave me an exhausted or maybe a pitying look. Then she softened. "Probably" was all she said.

I didn't get up from the bed. Eventually, Nanna reached for her phone and began pulling at her feed, smiling at the videos, and it seemed she was about to share a few memes with me. I was too exhausted and for a minute or two I nodded off. Then she got up, opened her closet, and removed her top and skirt. I watched as she slipped on a loose gray T-shirt.

"And how do you think Bjarke would feel about this?" I asked.

With her back turned to me, she said, "Bjarke is dead."

In the morning, when I walked into the kitchen, Nanna was seated at the bar with her computer, working on a campaign. Without looking up from the screen, she told me she'd made coffee and whisked up some eggs. I stood by the stove in front of her, buttering the pan, looking into her face, into her mouth and beautiful, unbending eyes, and for the first time in months, I felt terribly alive.

THE NEW MAITE

by YOHANCA DELGADO

NOW THAT SHE HAD her mornings to herself, Maite used them to drink coffee and stare at her naked body in the mirror. Using her hands as pincers, she clamped the new roll of fat near her belly with vicious force. Who was that sallow shadow? No scrutiny could explain why her body had betrayed her. She searched her scalp for dandruff. She clawed at her pores, carving an angry red half-moon into the side of her nose. She wandered into the living room in her underwear and blundered through a grainy eighties workout video she found on YouTube, only to give up halfway through. Padding to the window, she leaned past her own reflection to rest her forehead against the cold glass.

Outside, the bone-chilling winds of late fall seized Manhattan. Coursing through the trees, wrapping icy fingers around each green leaf and turning it to an ashy husk. These days were for being alone, for watching the gloomy onset of the season from the kitchen window.

But today, Maite was bored enough to take a walk. She cocooned herself in one sweater after another—three in total—before pulling on the maternity coat, the brick-colored quilted thing Cris wished she would put away already, because wouldn't people in the building talk? Maite stuffed her hands into the deep pockets—she couldn't care less what people said. The maternity coat was roomy, like a comforter with sleeves.

When she entered the Dunkin Donuts, she felt a heavenly frisson as her body acclimated to the new warmth and the smell of coffee and pastries—the purest pleasure in weeks. A sprinkling of customers loitered while a teenager stared at her phone behind the counter.

Maite had just settled in a corner with a coffee and a doughnut when the door opened and two women entered, bringing with them a gust of cold air.

Twins? Maite perked up, her eyes ping-ponging from one face to the other. But not just that: they were identically dressed in bubble-gum-pink puffy coats. Ethnically ambiguous and in their mid-thirties; short; with curvy bodies and hair an exultant shade of Barbie doll blond, wildly unnatural, long, and curled at the ends. At the first empty table, they wiggled out of their matching backpacks and placed the bags on the floor in unforced synchrony.

The women set about a long, complicated process of taking off their coats and getting settled across from each other. They watched each other placidly, the way one might watch one's own reflection.

Maite had read a news story once about a pair of twins who had grown up speaking a secret twin language. Until they were teenagers, they spoke only to each other. Then one of them apparently manipulated the other into committing suicide by convincing her that there could be only one, that only one of them could survive.

In the Dunkin Donuts, these twins stared at each other and did not speak. Maite watched them for what must have been a long time—until her cell phone chirped with a reminder to schedule a follow-up with her gynecologist.

"Come back in a month," the doctor had said. "Let's see how you feel, and go from there."

Cris had always been better than Maite at picking himself up and moving on. He'd already started talking again about their *family*, this abstract household crowded with fictive children.

Maite got up and disposed of her garbage. She bundled herself into the red coat and wound her scarf tightly around her neck. As she turned to walk out, something drew her gaze back to the twins.

They were watching her, both of them, with a sort of piercing interest that stripped Maite bare. She looked away and shrouded herself more tightly in her coat.

"Wait," one of them said, in a voice that sounded hoarse from disuse. She rose hurriedly and walked over to Maite, who paused, her whole body tensed, by the glass door.

"Sorry, what?"

"You can't ignore it," the twin said. The other twin, still in her seat, nodded. "She'll stay as long as it takes, but it ends here."

Shaking her head in confusion, Maite pushed the door open and rushed out into the street. Fucking weirdos, she thought. They get you every time.

Broadway was in its full afternoon hustle. Maite plunged her hands back into her coat pockets. The icy wind searched her bundled figure for entry points and found one at the exposed hollow of her throat, where her scarf had shifted. She shivered a bone-deep shiver, bowed her head, and set off toward home.

When she heard footsteps behind her, she walked faster.

The footsteps also quickened.

Wasn't it better to confront an attacker head-on? She pivoted on her heels, fists clenched.

"What do you want?"

The woman running up to her looked exactly like Maite, down to the brick red maternity coat, unzipped to reveal the same gray wool sweater Maite herself was wearing. The stranger's hair fluttered across her face as she caught up.

"It's you," the double said.

Maite took a step back. She had always hated the sound of her own voice. "Don't come any closer," she said. Her heart fluttered. Was she having some kind of hallucination? Had someone drugged her coffee?

"Okay, okay," the twin said in Maite's voice. She raised her palms.

Maite turned again and kept walking, faster. She had to get home and into bed. In her coat pocket, she wrapped her hand around her cell phone. She would outrun this weird mirage and call Cris.

She heard the footsteps behind her, uneven and persistent.

About halfway down the block, Maite whipped around again to look at the double, who stopped and let herself be examined. How was this possible? But there it was, her own face: the same ice pick scars on the cheekbone, the brassy highlights she was trying to grow out, a red crescent on the side of the double's nose. Maite's mouth went dry.

"What do you want," said Maite. No one else seemed to notice the two carbon copies standing in the middle of the sidewalk. An old woman in a heavy green coat dragged her wheelie grocery cart around them both.

"I'm not sure," the double said. "But I know you."

"Nope, sorry," said Maite. "You do not." She turned and kept walking, with the double in hapless pursuit.

A few paces later, Maite turned again. "Show me your forearm," she said.

Even though Maite hadn't specified which one, the twin immediately began rolling up her left coat sleeve, to reveal the words Maite had known she'd see there.

"Where did you get that tattoo," Maite barked. She remembered herself at nineteen in the East Village, head bowed as the green-haired tattoo artist pressed ink into each letter he had stenciled onto her skin, pausing to wipe the beads of blood away. On the stool next to hers, Cris held her other hand, his own tattoo already finished and covered in plastic wrap. To avoid the sight of blood, she had trained her eyes on their reflections in the shop-window, hers supine on the table, Cris's shoulders hunched at her side, the wobbly almost-palindrome OOTTAT arching over them in large Old English letters.

"I don't know," said the twin, in the frenetic daylight of Broadway. She scratched at the tattoo, as if to remove it. "I don't know, I don't know."

She looked imploringly at Maite. Maite stared back.

"Can I go with you," the double said, after what seemed like a long time. She tucked a wisp of hair into her mouth and sucked on it.

What a disgusting habit, Maite thought. I have to stop.

"No!" snapped Maite, horrified to think of this specter trailing her all the way home. She turned and walked fast, weaving her way easily through the crowd, with the double half running after her.

Against her better instincts, Maite looked back. The double moved through the crowds the way children do, bumping into people and blithely continuing on her way without thinking to apologize or correct her trajectory.

"Watch it!" a tall woman shouted when the double knocked a gallon of milk out of her gloved hand. Her clumsiness was stunning to Maite—how could someone be this bad at getting down the street?

Maite sped up. One good thing about the city: you could easily lose someone.

She resolved to stop turning back, but when she was forced to wait at the next crosswalk, she listened for the double's uncontrolled run.

Heeding a sudden instinct, Maite swung her arm back in a tree-chopping motion—just in time to keep the twin from darting into the street. A yellow cab let out a long honk as it careened by. Next to Maite, the double bent at the waist, put her hands on her knees, and panted. Her hair dropped over her face.

"Jesus," said Maite. "You have to watch where you're going."

The twin straightened up again, nodding fast.

Maite didn't have to think for long to imagine all the horrible things that New York could do to a woman who looked and behaved like this and had nowhere to go.

"Do you speak Spanish?" she asked, still brusque, though no longer so harsh.

The double shook her head.

"You're going to need it." The light changed and Maite started walking again, slower this time, so the twin could keep up.

Back at the apartment, the twin wandered from room to room, touching everything Maite loved. She brushed her fingers over the photo of Maite and Cris cutting their wedding cake, the sparkly dresses hanging in the closet, the beat-up laptop, the dog-eared poetry books shelved in the living room. Then the two Maites faced off in the kitchen and stripped off sweater after sweater, until they were down to their identical white Hanes T-shirts. Maite opened a frosty Presidente for each of them and leaned across the table.

"What's your name?"

"Maite."

"What's your date of birth?"

"I don't know."

"Who are your parents?"

"I don't know."

"Where were you yesterday?"

"Yesterday? I only know about today."

"Okay, what's your earliest memory?"

"I was running down the street to catch you. It was important."

"To who?"

"To me."

"Why?"

"I don't know."

"Where were you before that?"

"I don't know."

"Are you a dream?"

"I don't think so. Are you?"

"Why are you here? What do you want?"

"I don't know. I don't know. I don't know." It turned out that the twin cried easily. Maite watched her with fascination, noting the way her face contorted.

"Have you ever been pregnant?"

"No," said the twin, draining her beer. Maite saw the identical gold wedding band on her ring finger. "Can I have another one?"

Maite was in the living room watching her double watch *Coco* when Cris's key turned in the door.

"That's my husband," Maite whispered to her wide-eyed double. "Wait here."

Maite cornered Cris in the hallway and told him what had happened, breathlessly: "She looks just like me, has my tattoo, I couldn't leave her alone…" When he shook his head in helpless bewilderment, she pulled him into the living room.

The new Maite leaned forward on the couch and shook Cris's limp hand with comical enthusiasm. He looked at the stranger and then at Maite. He stepped back, knocked over a vase, then righted it. "What the fuck is this," he said.

"She doesn't seem to have any memories," said Maite.

The twin nodded amiably.

"Again—what—where did you find this… this person?"

"On Broadway! Right outside Dunkin Donuts," Maite said, suddenly feeling defensive. "She followed me."

"Okay." Cris took a deep breath and let it out. He looked at the double. "You found a clone of yourself at Dunkin Donuts."

"I don't know if she's a clone, but that's where I found her. Maite, stop chewing your hair."

Maite stopped chewing her hair.

Cris whisked Maite out into the hallway. "We don't know what—or who—this... this person is," he said. "I wish you'd talked to me before you brought her into our house."

"Well, what did you want me to do, Cris? Leave her in the street?"

"Maybe," he said, his voice low and steady. "She's a stranger, and that's where you found her."

"Look at her," Maite said. The double sat on the couch, rubbing her tattoo with a fingertip. "She clearly needs to be here. I couldn't just leave her behind."

At dinner, Cris stared at them over his untouched plate.

"Why do we have this tattoo?" asked the twin.

"One of us fancied himself a poet," Maite said, pointing her chin at Cris, who mutely brandished the line of dark text on his own forearm and then wagged his fork in sarcastic celebration. "And the other one was in love."

"So you both have the same one! What does it mean?"

"It's about love," Maite said, as a wave of desperate sadness washed over her. "About us. We got them before we got married."

"What is 'married'?" asked the twin.

When Cris looked at her, Maite blinked hard, took a huge bite of steak, and pointed helplessly at her mouth.

Cris shrugged. "You mean besides the magic you see here?" He paused. "Do you know what sex is?"

"No," the twin said, tipping her head to one side. "What is it?"

"We can talk about it later," Maite blurted. "It's not that interesting."

Cris gave Maite a wounded look.

"I mean—people don't usually talk about it at dinner. It's considered bad manners."

"Because it's bad," offered the double, nodding solemnly.

Cris laughed and tipped the neck of his beer at Maite. "Not bad, just... only for making babies. With calendars and timers and everything."

The double looked from Maite to Cris, then took a long swig of her beer.

"That's right," Maite said, her voice sharper than it needed to be. "Takes two to live that way, though, doesn't it?"

Cris sawed at his steak. Maite ignored the familiar burn in her cheeks. She turned and watched for several silent minutes as the twin clumsily taught herself to eat the exact way Maite did: fork tines down, knife in the left hand. She wasn't watching Maite, either, but acting on some latent instinct.

"Do you have any?" asked the double. "Babies?" Several pieces of yellow corn tumbled from her mouth and onto the tablecloth.

"Not quite," Maite said, too brightly.

Cris raised his eyebrows at Maite and then leaned over to pick up the corn with a paper towel. His wedding ring glinted in the kitchen light.

"Sorry, Cris," Maite said. "How was work today?"

"Nothing that hasn't been said before, right? Today was fine," Cris said. "Quarterly tax deadlines in a month, companies showing up with the equivalent of a garbage bag full of crumpled receipts. But more overtime for us, so there's that."

"I'm sorry. I'm going back to work soon and maybe you can take some leave—unpaid, even—and be at home, like I got to be."

He waved his hand. "Don't worry about that."

They spent the rest of the dinner in silence until the twin asked Maite why they, the two Maites, looked equally old when she herself was so new.

"This is shampoo," Maite said, opening the shower curtain as the running water began to warm the bathroom. "For your hair. This bar is soap, for your body. Are you listening to me?"

She looked back and saw that the new Maite was naked. It was all there: the flaccid, empty belly; the cellulite; the tattoo; the appendectomy scar; the large, uneven breasts.

Ashamed, Maite averted her eyes.

"You can look if you want," the double said in a stage whisper. "We have the same body and it's working pretty great so far." Heeding some odd impulse, the twin did a clumsy naked pirouette. Maite laughed, from deep in her belly.

"Let's do a bath," she said to the twin and put the stopper in the old tub.

As the twin marveled at the foamy wonders of the bubble bath, Maite went to the baby's room. It was the first time she had entered the room in over a month, though she must have walked by it hundreds of times, stopping every now and then to listen at the door, half expecting to hear a tiny cry.

She and Cris had painted the walls dove gray. The crib was a hand-me-down from his sister and had a new bumper and linens inside, still in their plastic wrappings. Next to the crib stood a small bed. They hadn't even started on the decorations. It had been too early. It pained her to see the single stuffed animal, a little lion, gathering dust on the small white dresser.

Cris found her and sat down next to her on the bed.

"We'll try again, Mitty," he said.

"Stop saying that."

"Stop walling me out. I lost a baby too."

Maite pursed her lips and said nothing.

"I can't say I feel exactly what you feel, Maite. But I'm mourning too."

He awkwardly put an arm around her shoulder. She let him.

"I'm afraid," she said. "What if it happens again?" She let her head drop against Cris's chest.

"It might," said Cris. "I think we have to decide if we're willing to take that risk."

"What if I'm not willing to take that risk? Am I a coward?"

"No," Cris said. "Just human. People are allowed to be scared."

Maite stared at a white noise machine, still in its packaging. *How do you go on?*

Her heart could not see beyond the question. It did not matter what everyone believed.

After the first miscarriage, she had picked herself up and continued. She had returned to her job in admin the day after her body began to expel that fiction, a child she had allowed herself to love. She had been chipper on the phone; she had made jokes! Even when you could no longer trust yourself, you could force your body to go through the motions of living.

It turned out you could even create a new life a few short months later. And you could refuse to go to the hospital when the bleeding started. You could pace the apartment in panicked denial for several hours instead, only to end up there anyway, relinquishing yet another life you had failed to protect. Maybe you were bottomless. Maybe you could take *that* grief, too, and grind it down into something leaden and small and deadly. Maybe you could keep going and pretend it had not pierced a vital artery.

"None of it is your fault," Cris said. She studied the tensed muscles in his jaw. It dawned on her that she was not the only ailing thing. She turned his forearm and brushed the tips of her fingers over his tattoo. After ten years of seeing it every day, it still surprised her: the way the words, unbidden, sometimes asserted themselves in her consciousness: BETWEEN THE SHADOW AND THE SOUL.

"I'd better go check that she hasn't drowned in the tub," she said, rising to her feet. "Not sure I'm equipped to deal with a dead clone."

Maite spread a clean, pale pink fitted sheet on the bed in the baby's room as the twin—now squeaky-clean and clad in Maite's old college sweatpants—hovered behind her. The sheets had been for when her mother and Tia Gladys came to help with the baby. Maite fluffed a pillow in its new pink case.

She held up one end of the coverlet and the twin scrambled in, pressing her face against the fresh sheets. Maite sat on the edge of the bed and stared at this strange, innocent version of herself, clutching the stuffed lion. Is this what she looked like when she was happy? The double smiled. Her dimples showed. This guileless stranger would take some getting used to.

Maite smiled back at the woman in her baby's room. Without thinking, she kissed the new Maite on the forehead. She plugged in a star-shaped night-light and left the door open for her, in case she felt afraid. The swaddled form seemed so defenseless in the dark.

"Goodbye!" the twin called out.

"Goodnight," Maite said.

Maite walked through the apartment, turning off lights as she went. She decided that she wanted, fiercely, to keep the double here. To study herself before she learned to be afraid. But she worried for this free-floating stranger, empty as she was of memory. Such lightness. Not cleaved to the earth, as Maite was.

Maite shivered as she climbed into bed beside Cris, who rolled over in his sleep and draped an arm over her. Outside their bedroom window, the wind howled. The cold found its way into the apartment, pushing icy tendrils through some unseen opening.

In the days that followed, the twin proved to be a quick study. She was both empty and bottomless, gathering information everywhere. At first, Maite watched her constantly, terrified that she would hurt herself. But it wasn't necessary.

The double learned Spanish practically over-night from watching telenovelas on Univision. By the time Maite went back to work that Monday, the twin had learned the basics of cooking from YouTube.

And it took only a few days to find a routine: Maite and Cris set off for work, and the twin spent the day learning and cleaning. With a kind of grudging admiration, Cris brought out an old sous vide device, and the double made perfect buttery steaks.

One day, the double asked for a set of spare keys and began going for long runs along Riverside Drive and stopping for groceries on the way home.

Meanwhile, the real Maite sleepwalked through the workday, then commuted home, where her like-ness waited to serve elaborate dinners, and then, brimming with energy, regale her and Cris with rambling catalogs of all the things she had learned that day. Maite listened with beaming pride seamed with a growing unease.

Cris warmed to the double's presence. Sometimes Maite even heard the two of them talking without her. The double took an interest in everything Cris liked. She could recite whole poems by Neruda now. She claimed to understand the tattoo.

"'I love you without knowing how, or when, or from where,'" Maite heard the double say to herself, as she washed the dishes. "'I love you straightforwardly, without complexities or pride.'"

One morning, a few weeks after the double arrived, Maite woke to the sound of the front door closing and realized she had overslept. Disoriented, she reached for her phone and saw that it was missing from her bedside table. Cursing under her breath, she jumped up and got dressed while trying to remember where she'd put her workbag.

When it finally occurred to her to look out the window, she glimpsed the twin jauntily turning the corner onto Broadway, Maite's workbag hanging from her shoulder.

Maite yanked on a pair of sneakers and scrambled out the door, sprinting the three blocks to the subway, where the double stood on the platform in Maite's red coat, slacks, and heels, scrolling on Maite's phone.

"Hey!" Maite shouted, slamming into the turnstile as the downtown 1 train pulled into the station.

The double seemed genuinely surprised to see her. "I'm going to be late," she shouted over the screech of the wheels as they came to a stop. She stepped into the car.

"Wait!" Maite hopped the turnstile just as the doors closed.

The double smiled and waved from the window as the train rumbled out of the station.

Maite sprinted out of the station to hail a taxi. She would intercept the double before she got to her office on Sixty-Second Street. Then she remembered that she had no phone, no wallet, no office ID to scan to get into the building. Who would believe her? And what if the double meant no harm? Was it worth causing some reality-TV-style argument at work? Wasn't Maite keeping this job only for the maternity leave, anyway?

On the walk home, Maite had to remind herself to put one foot in front of the other, while the city crowds hustled on, a blur of noise and color passing her by. She imagined the double on the subway, then at her own desk, bantering with her coworkers. The key felt heavy as she let herself back into the building and rode the slow, creaky elevator back up to the apartment. Maite watched the clock, her mind dashing, with each tick of the second hand, between the notion of locking the double into the apartment forever—and the notion of locking her out of it.

The twin came home in a gust of cold air, seeming both stronger and somehow taller, and carrying a bag full of groceries. Ignoring Maite, she kicked off her shoes and began to make dinner. Maite, who had been lying in wait, glowered at the twin from the kitchen table as she whisked around the kitchen, unpacking things and, with her back to Maite, dicing tomatoes and deboning a chicken.

After watching for a few furious, speechless minutes, Maite found herself standing next to the double. "Are we going to talk about what you did this morning? What the fuck do you think you're playing at?"

With deft fingers, the double found the bird's joints and cut them open to find a bone. She tore off a wing, then a leg. She flipped the chicken onto the other side and paused.

"Admit it," the double said, turning to face Maite. Knife in one hand and chicken in the other, she rubbed her nose with the back of her wrist. "I did what you wanted."

Maite felt the truth of this, though she didn't fully understand it. Her shoulders dropped. All temporary, she said to herself. The realization soothed her, though the words felt strange, as if written by someone else. It is what I wanted. As sure as a change in seasons.

"No," Maite said. "I never told you I wanted you to take my place. Do you hear me?"

Was the double even listening? Using the knife tip, she pierced the bird's sternum. She pulled out the breastbone with a sharp crack and tossed it aside.

"Look, Maite," the double said. She cleaved the unprotected breast in two, as naturally as if she'd been doing it all her life. The blade flashed in her hand. Bits of flesh speckled her bloodied fingers. "You decide how this ends."

"What?"

"You heard me," the double said, returning to the chicken. She zigzagged the knife in the air.

"Make a decision. I didn't choose your life, but someone has to live it."

This wasn't how it was supposed to go. The old Maite waited for Cris to get home, lurking in the bedroom beneath a pile of blankets, like one of those alligators she'd seen on the news, biding their time before emerging darkly from some neglected Florida marsh, only to be flattened in traffic.

She heard his key in the door and bristled as he made small talk with the double, his easy laugh cascading down the hallway that separated the kitchen from the bedroom. Maite pounced on him as soon as he turned the bedroom doorknob, loosening his tie with his free hand.

"Heyyy, Mitty-mitty," he said, pulling her close.

Maite swatted him away and rushed to lock the door. "She's out of control," she whispered. "She went to my job. She waved a knife at me!"

Cris frowned. "She did *what*?"

"She's going to kill me, I think!"

"Slow down—you think she's dangerous?" He

sat her down on the bed and kneeled before her, scanning her body for injuries. "Are you okay?"

"I'm fine, I'm fine."

"You always say that. But—and don't get mad at me—*are* you?"

"Only one of us is going to make it," said Maite. "She says I decide."

"Okay, well, that's just... lunacy, Maite. If you decide you don't want her here, we can take her somewhere... a women's shelter or something, I don't know— Oh, Mitty, don't cry. What do you want?" He kissed her tear-lined face. "I'll do whatever makes you happy."

Here it was, a realization heavy enough to make her wish she could crack open her own rib cage wide enough to pry it out and cast it aside.

"She's me, isn't she? Better, happy."

Cris shook his head. "If I could take this weight off your shoulders, Mitty, and carry it alone, I would."

"Is that a threat or a promise?"

He tiredly wiped a thumb across her cheek. "It's both and it's neither, Maite. You know that."

*　　*　　*

So the old Maite marooned herself on the couch and let the double do the work of living. The twin did it easily, too, cycling through the days—which seemed to quicken as the sun set earlier and earlier—happily and with a vigor the old Maite had never possessed.

Cris, meanwhile, avoided the double, warily sidestepping her attempts to make conversation. Sometimes, when the double was doing the dishes, he stared at Maite with a lost, suffocated expression that Maite ignored. It got easier, over time, to ignore all of it. And there was the double, waiting in the wings, ready to pick up wherever she left off.

But when the double appeared at the threshold of her bedroom one night, in a satiny slip Maite thought she had thrown away a long time ago, Maite threw off the covers and planted both feet on the floor. Beside her, Cris snored quietly.

The new Maite stepped into the room, her familiar silhouette backlit by the light in the hallway, and the old Maite rose to meet her, heart pounding under her sweatshirt, wondering if this was the moment, if this was the line.

At first glance, the new Maite was alien enough to be almost beautiful, lips slicked in a color Maite used to love, hair tumbled around her shoulders in abundant, glossy curls, a halo of the perfume Maite used to wear. But no, there they were, the haunted ridges and pores of her own face, the three tiny craters on her cheekbone.

The old Maite stood transfixed. What had she, the old Maite, meant to do? The double smiled and the old Maite could feel the edges of her own lips rising to mirror hers, though she didn't feel like smiling. The double stepped around her and walked to the bed.

The old Maite wanted to scream, to tackle the double and rip her hair out. But she was rooted to the ground. She watched the double climb in and pull the blankets up around herself. Watched Cris roll over, still in his sleep, and wrap his arms around the double.

How long did she stand there? Long enough for her anger to become something else, a sort of stupor, and for it to turn her gently by the shoulders and guide her to the baby's room, where it laid her down on the twin bed and dispatched her into a night of deep sleep.

* * *

In the morning, she pulled up a chair at the breakfast table with the new Maite and Cris, who giggled at some joke she'd just missed. They clinked coffee cups—and as an afterthought, tapped their cups against the old Maite's empty one.

This is the moment, the old Maite thought. She wanted to flip the table, send the strawberry-topped waffles flying across the room. She wanted to pummel the new Maite with her fists. She willed herself to do it.

But she sat and stared at Cris instead. He made a point of meeting her eyes and smiling at her, then looking quickly away, as if he couldn't bear it. He dropped an ice cube into his hot coffee to cool it down.

"Listen," the new Maite said brightly, turning to the old Maite. "I don't have to be at work until ten today. Want to go for a walk?"

That she was being patronized was not lost on the old Maite, but she nodded mutely. The two of them put on their red coats and set off for Dunkin Donuts—where else?—for coffee. The old Maite watched the new Maite without self-conscious-ness. She felt anger, yes, but also an obliterating tenderness.

At Dunkin Donuts, the new Maite stared at her doughnut and pushed it over to the old Maite.

"You have it. I forgot that I already ate."

The old Maite ate both doughnuts gratefully, with a hunger that surprised her. All the while, the new Maite shifted in her seat, crossing and recross-ing her legs, adjusting an unfamiliar silk blouse. Finally, she looked at her watch.

"I've got to get back," the new Maite said. While the new Maite gathered up the garbage and carried it to the trash can, the old Maite began to cry. She put her head in her arms and sobbed into the sleeves of the maternity coat. Full, body-wracking grief. Loud, too, but no one in the Dunkin Donuts turned to watch, not the employee restocking the doughnuts with metal tongs, not the goth teenager in giant headphones, not the fur-clad woman mur-muring to herself as she stirred her coffee.

The new Maite paused by the trash can and watched the huddled form. She closed her eyes for a long moment. It was time. She strode back purposefully and squeezed old Maite's shoulder, kissed the top of her head.

"Goodbye," whispered the new Maite. But she wasn't sure if any of it registered with the old Maite's heaving shoulders. That's how the new Maite would always remember her, weeping in that coat in that Dunkin Donuts. It seemed she would never stop crying. Who knows? Maybe she never did.

Maite had just enough time to stop at home for her office ID and hop on the downtown 1. Where did she keep the other winter coats? How had it not occurred to her to ditch this baggy thing? She needed something lighter, sleeker. She unzipped the big red coat to let the cold air in and quick-stepped into the bustle of Broadway.

Dead winter now, heavy velvet clouds overhead, a promise of rain. Her life was gathering speed. The marriage would not last.

She walked fast. The icy air pinkened her cheeks. It is so much easier to weave through the crowd, she realized, when you're alone and do not need to look back.

THE STARLIGHT

by LYDIA CONKLIN

AFTER WORK ON THURSDAY, Martin returns to his tidy, cramped room in a corner of the Starlight Co-op. The day's debugging and code development slip away. His eyes, after hours of anxious squinting, bloom open as he removes his work shirt and polyester pants and dons a cloth robe, his required uniform for the Community Sex Act.

He should be nervous as he tucks his shoulders into the fabric—he's now lived in the co-op for three weeks, and his STI screening has just come through—but he's not. He cinches the sash and peers into the mirror. His face is unlined, though he's thirty-eight years old. He can't believe nearly four decades of life have passed, because in his heart he's seventeen. He sinks a finger into his cheek, which hasn't changed texture since childhood. The girls will watch him closely tonight, at his first Sex Act. Especially, he hopes, Winnie, though her focus will be hardest to catch. Sometimes she digs into him with her stare, which travels over his face and neck, down his shoulders, and across the mound of his belly—sizing him up—but more often she looks out above him, through the window or at the wall, her face tightening as worries seem to bubble up and pass. She carries with her a sorrow that Martin has managed only to glimpse in moments. He's not sure where it comes from, but he longs to draw close to it, to comfort her.

Out his window, behind a spiky tangle of cacti, the girls in their white robes have gathered by the fountain full of clear blue marbles. Winnie steers the backs of June and Sarah-Beth, gripping so firmly that the blood drains from her big white hands. Sarah-Beth strains to look over Winnie's shoulder and through the yucca to the traffic on El Camino, maybe the karate center across the street, the burrito takeout beside it, or the flimsy storefront bar, her face sagging with want. June bends away from Winnie's hand, skinny arms swinging. Winnie herds them back together, her noble face collapsing, even from this distance. She speaks so intensely that her shoulders bob, her elbows. Her forehead strains and wrinkles.

Winnie is a handsome, upstanding professional who never would've looked at Martin in regular life. They first met in a coffee shop in Mountain View over a month ago. She took her time settling into the seat across from him—she was fifty or so, black hair punished into a bun, clothing dark and fibrous and expensive. Despite the severe beauty of her sturdy face and broad, strong hands, she radiated a warm calm, and he already regretted how short the meeting would be. She told him he looked different from how she'd expected.

"Different how?" he asked.

She paused before allowing, "Younger."

Martin had found her post on Craigslist:

Seeking male virgin, 35+, for semipermanent roommate arrangement in College Terrace, Palo

Alto. We are an intentional community working under principles of safety, healing, and radical care. No pets.

He imagined adult virgins looming over terrariums of snakes or lizards, cooling the burning in their pants by running their hands over scaly skin, wishing to feel softness, body heat, imagining the scales melting down into human flesh. He has the rats, sure, but that's not the same. He doesn't like them that way.

Martin followed up on the ad—he told himself—out of innocent curiosity, and discovered several key facets of the arrangement. First, the apartment was rent-free. Additionally, the girls prepared "energy-renewing quasi-raw vegetarian meals on a biweekly basis." He pictured passing bowls of beets and carrots to open-handed, intelligent women who would actually talk to him, who'd set their hands on his shoulder as they stood from the table, pushing themselves up, affectionate, mischievous, a club of happy ghosts ushering him into a world free of all the old anxieties. Friendship, it seemed, was the key to the co-op, even though, in these first weeks, at least, he's failed to seize it. And then there were the erotic duties.

In his correspondence about the ad, he'd tried to be coy, hadn't wanted to ask outright. He was only emailing for fun, anyway. He wouldn't really meet Winnie, much less accept the offer. But as the days passed and Winnie kept appearing in his in-box, her messages always charming and prompt and detailed, as though responding to him were her primary pleasure in life, Martin considered more closely his outdated condo rental in Menlo Park, off the Safeway parking lot, with Clive and the rat colony. The rats had bred by accident, multiplying until they needed a second terrarium, then a third. Martin enjoyed stroking the creatures, and liked feeling that he was never alone. He especially liked hearing a scrabbling in the apartment that wasn't Clive marching around to his favorite jazz, but there was the smell, and soon the numbers swelled to the point where Martin didn't want to tell anyone how many he had.

"How they doing?" Carla, his office manager, had asked a few months ago. "You got a hundred?"

"Not yet," Martin said, blushing. Carla looked like his high school sweetie, Hannah Bernhardt. Both women moved carefully, picking their way through the air like it was gel. "But," he told her, "at this rate, it won't be long."

Martin's first three weeks at the co-op have been lonesome. Winnie warned him that the girls might visit him for comfort, but no one has. He's approached them on his own—Sarah-Beth, while she perched on the stoop sunning her naked back; June, while she read in the communal area. June remained spacey and remote when he approached, clutching her skinny arms around her like she was sick, while Sarah-Beth laughed in his face, her giant blond head half-cheerful and half-mean, eyes sharp and bright, telling him how bizarre he was, how she couldn't believe what came out of his mouth. Mostly he sits beside the girls where he finds them, stammering out a few attempts as they grow stiffer, glancing around for an out, eventually excusing themselves. At mealtimes they talk amongst themselves—an animated trio—while

Martin picks at the vegetarian offering, Winnie tall and straight and distracted at the distant end of the table. Sometimes she scribbles notes. He hopes the Sex Act, which occurs every Thursday, will bring them together. A couple of Sex Acts have already occurred since he's been here, but this is the first to which he's been invited.

Yesterday after work, Winnie coached him on the philosophy and logistics of the Community Sex Act. Leaning against the door jamb of his room in her work blazer, she reviewed the birth control pills, the frequent disease screenings, the standards of hygiene, while he lay on the bed, cowed by her arresting frame.

"Our girls have been through difficult situations," she said, her voice heavy, like she hated to share the news. "Sexually speaking."

"Like what?"

"I'm sorry, no." Her hands flattened against the air. "Those details are reserved for women-only Sharing Meetings."

"Of course," Martin said, though everything about the co-op was new. Having a woman in his room was new. He squeezed the pillow in his arms. Winnie was protective of the girls and her methods. The handbook explained how she'd been a court-appointed social worker for a decade, which Martin couldn't fathom. One day she'd run into an old client at a bar and came to understand how much damage she'd inflicted over the years, minimizing women's stories, only half listening, retraumatizing them and directing them into a system that brutalized them further. Winnie wanted to build a space "as unlike the criminal justice system as imaginable," where "friendship, caring, and healing are overlords of all activity." The booklet claimed she'd aided several dozen women with her "self-taught, unorthodox methods," and that she'd never rest "until forced to by age or untimely death."

"Are you absorbing this, Martin?" Winnie asked.

"Yes."

"Your purpose is to be grateful for whatever our girls can give. You're supposed to do this without prompting, but we all know real life isn't so smooth. We've had, shall we say, 'issues' in the past, so I want to be up front. And, Martin"—her eyelashes lowered—"there's no need to indicate we had this talk."

"Got it." Martin nodded to press the point.

"Your job is to work quickly and with gratitude." Martin wished she'd sit next to him. He longed to feel her heat through the bedclothes. "Brief and kind is what they can stand. And there's the community aspect, of course. We're reinventing sex as a joy shared with friends in a protected environment. By the time I bring these girls to you, of course, we've already gone through several rounds of intensive group therapy, and performed preliminary Sex Acts without you. So it's not like they're raw." Her voice grew rich. "They're in good shape, all three of them. They're on their way. But you can never be too sensitive."

"Got it."

Winnie regarded Martin with scrutiny, as she must have her clients in the cold, green-lit rooms of police stations in downtown San Jose. She tapped her forehead. "Keep this in mind: you're a burst of joy."

Martin opened his hands in a gesture that he hoped looked festive, but Winnie wrinkled her face.

"I'm going to request that you attend to Kate

first. She's been around the longest and will set the tone."

That was a relief. Martin was most comfortable talking to Kate, who resembled an aging college student: cardigans, a tight braid, bright responses framed to please. But sometimes he got the sense she spoke as though from a script: she'd had a career once; she believed in this process; she savored the comfort of a solid dog.

"Do your thing, then progress to the others in turn."

As Winnie stepped out the door with her stiff walk, panic squeezed Martin's heart. She was leaving, but he didn't have enough information. "How should I do it, though?"

"What do you mean?"

"What style of lovemaking?" He could be soft and affectionate; he could be rough like in the movies. And there were positions too. She hadn't given him enough information.

Winnie's face melted in tenderness. "Just feel it out, okay? The procedure should take about twenty-five minutes. Just focus on the time: twenty-five minutes."

"I understand." He had no idea what she was talking about, but she spoke with such confidence, her face so lit up, that he lost the heart to question her.

Clive hadn't been too thrilled last month when Martin announced he was moving; he'd claimed Martin was responsible for 50 percent of the rats. In answer, Martin had produced Winnie's ad, dragging his cursor to highlight the clearly described policy against pets.

"You little shit," Clive said. "You're moving to a sex house."

"It's not a sex house."

"You should've told me. You totally have my blessing, bro-man."

Clive's words make Martin nervous now. So far the Starlight hasn't felt like a sex house, but more like a waiting room, people's limbs tensed for the moment their names will be called. The girls defer to Winnie as if she were a dorm mother, and she wanders solitary among them, offering compliments on their hair or the tidiness of their ensembles. They accept these remarks with a nod and a server's smile.

On his first day, Winnie showed Martin the placards around the co-op that helped facilitate conversation and friendship: signs about body language and intimacy and opening compliments. One said: CONCENTRATE AT ALL MOMENTS ON BEING NATURAL. Just reading the sign stiffened Martin's spine. That night, the group had enjoyed invigorating lentil stew with tempeh sausage. Martin glanced around the table, picturing Kate and June embroiled in the passion of the Community Sex Act, Sarah-Beth amusing herself on the sidelines, giggling at the activity, boldly stroking between her legs. June was tiny, with a lined face and a thick fountain of shiny doll's hair, body tensely coiled in her seat. All he could extract from her in their friendship chats was that she was older than the others, that she had a kid who was in college, and that she was studying, late in life, to be a humanitarian lawyer. Kate sat with her shoulders back, yellow cardigan smooth over her chest, like she was being pressed by some authority to look at ease. Martin feared even approaching her. And

Sarah-Beth was too loose, hands flapping in the air, her laugh so loud it set the other girls on edge. In those initial weeks, Martin had tried Sarah-Beth several times for friendship—she was the most gregarious of the women—and their conversations had lasted the longest. She'd been wild, she'd confided, and would be again one day. Her sister had encouraged this spell at the Starlight because of "a hard thing at a party once"—she'd said it with a wave of her hand, like she didn't care. She couldn't stomach all this quiet.

That night hadn't been quiet, though. The girls had chatted about their cruel managers, their aching feet, by turns skittish and, as the meal progressed, generously, sweetly intimate, Kate leaning against Sarah-Beth's broad shoulder—theirs was the closest alliance—and glancing at Winnie for the occasional maternal nod. Only June seemed ill at ease, shifting her shoulders and kicking the air, checking the door like she expected visitors. Over dessert, Kate had described a particularly nasty party of Swedes she'd served. One Swede had scolded her for not smiling, another had refused his pork, while a third had raised his wineglass so aggressively for a refill that the lip of the glass bit her chin. She tapped the cut: a perfect red dash.

"Oh, but it's hot on you," said Sarah-Beth. "Makes you look tough."

"Well, I don't know," said Kate, looking down with a crooked smile.

"None of that," snapped Winnie.

"Sorry," said Kate. "Sorry, sorry. We didn't mean it." She touched the little red window into her face, like she planned to cover it with her finger until it healed.

"What's wrong with liking a cut?" June asked. "It doesn't mean anything." Her face narrowed, birdlike, challenging.

"Never mind," said Winnie, and swept away their plates.

Later that night, in his closet, Martin lifted a piece of hole-punched tinfoil off one of the cowboy boots Clive had given him for his birthday. Inside the toe were two rats, curled with their feet on each other's bellies. The girls would be angry if they knew, but just as he was moving out of the condo, he'd glimpsed the terrariums. All that life was his responsibility. He'd reached a hand between the roiling bodies, heartbeats slapping his palm. He meant only to offer a final stroke, but when his hand came up, two rats were attached. They weren't even his favorites, but they were the ones who wanted him. He hadn't had the heart to deny them.

As he cradled the rats and considered his soon-to-depart virginity, voices mumbled in the hall. Martin stuffed the rats into his boot and opened the door a little.

June and Kate leaned against the wall twenty feet away. Their faces pressed together as they whispered. They didn't notice him.

"I know what you're saying," Kate said. "Trust me, I felt that way too. For a long time."

"The Healing Process?" June squeezed her endless ponytail. "I mean, is she serious?"

"Completely." Kate leaned toward June. Maybe because their training had involved sex with each other, the girls had developed a bodily ease with one another that Martin had never enjoyed in any friendship. He envied it. "She's dead serious," Kate went on. "All the weird shit—it's all her. But she cares, genuinely. And the method works. Not the fluffy crap. But the heart."

"You're still here," June said. "So it didn't work for you."

"It absolutely worked for me," Kate snapped. "You don't know what I went through."

"I do."

"You don't. Because you can never understand unless some shit like that happens to you." She raised her hands, half in apology, half in defense. "Look. It's not a competition. But you didn't know me a month ago. I couldn't have even referenced what happened. I couldn't have touched another human." She squeezed June's shoulder. "Swallow the cheesy shit and try." She made a low sound in her throat. So the Starlight was helping Kate. Martin stood straighter against the door. "Anything's better than what's out there."

"Martin?" Sarah-Beth had stepped into Martin's blind spot, beside his door. She loomed tall, her skeleton dense and sturdy, pushing the skin at her cheekbones and knees. "Are you watching Kate? That's naughty."

"It's all right, SB," said Kate. "He's part of the group."

"He's eavesdropping?" June's voice went high and thin.

"Would you like to join me for a snack, June?" Martin asked. "Is now an appropriate time to make such a proposal?"

"Ugh," June said, turning to Kate. "Do you see what I mean? How is this not so awkward?"

She stormed away, Kate following. Martin's throat swelled and closed as they disappeared. He longed to call them back, but that would seem aggressive.

"Can I come in?" Sarah-Beth was already halfway into Martin's room, blond hair shaggy behind her ears, forehead pink with attention. Maybe Martin could befriend Sarah-Beth first, and then she, with all her lubricated gestures, could ingratiate him to the others. She gifted him a smile. A good start. "You're struggling, Martin. Do you want a tip?"

Martin stood in front of the closet, blocking the scrambling of the rats. "That'd be cool." He was terrified of the Sex Act, and would accept any guidance offered.

Sarah-Beth tapped her fingers along her arm. "Look. It's sweet that you want to be friends. But that's not what we need."

"What do you need?" His voice was too high.

"We need someone to be sexy. Kinky, even. All these stupid groups we have every five seconds? Our sessions or whatever?" She swirled her hand over her head. "I know more about these girls' sex lives than I know about my own."

"Okay." He tried not to betray his disbelief, molding his face into an expression of neutrality.

"You don't know how things work, but that's part of the point. We have weird shit. Get it?"

He fidgeted, willing her to leave. "I get it."

Her overlarge mouth stretched disapprovingly. He wasn't convincing her. "That's why none of the other guys worked before: they were oh-so-tender. If normal shit turned us on, would we be here? Waiting around for some random old guy?"

"I guess not."

"No. The answer is no."

*   *   *

Martin cheerleads himself as he heads downstairs for the Community Sex Act, the yucca a spiky shadow looming out the window. He reviews his plan: Kate first, quickly and with gratitude. He's lucky she's first, because she's made progress, she trusts the process, and so starting with her will be comforting. Then the other three. Twenty-five minutes. That's six and a quarter minutes for each person—or maybe he'll go faster early, spend the spare time on Winnie.

The lobby of the co-op, which the girls call the Sharing Room, is sunlit and quiet. They've cleaned specially. The pillows on the daybed neatly overlap. The Starlight's sign, with its orange constellations and inclusive nighttime rainbow, has been adjusted to a jaunty angle on the coffee table. The fruit bowl, delicate as spun sugar, cradles a single ripe banana. Martin has never seen the house so empty. Normally the girls are sipping water and reading, talking to one another, tapping rhythms on the armrests. Their phones have all been quarantined.

Winnie's bedroom is in the back of the house. He saw a sliver of it on his tour, but the door has been sealed ever since. He knocks. There's a muffled snort. And then Sarah-Beth says, "Come in, Martin." She pronounces his name sarcastically.

He takes a breath and swings the door wide. Everything is white here: bedspread, pillows, a wicker chair, the walls.

Winnie and Sarah-Beth are on the bed, cross-legged. June is on the wicker chair. The chair is outsize, and she's shrunken in it, her chocolate ponytail fountaining to the side, so long it tickles the floor. Kate is on the carpet, the only part of the room that's been dirtied into off-white, darkest in the path from door to bed. She sits up straight, hands firm on her knees.

The girls are clothed, their robes folded in a stack by the door. Martin had pictured them nude, heads poking out in a row from the bedspread, like an illustration in a kids' book. With that setup, he could swiftly dip into each. If he's being honest with himself, this obligation was what most appealed to him about the Starlight. Not the free rent and parking, not the good peninsula location, not shedding the barnyard reek of too many rats. Not even having four women to laugh with and talk to, though that benefit comes second. He knows how situations like this end, knows about Waco and Charles Manson. What drew him to the Starlight was the promise of getting his first time over with through obligation. Where he couldn't back out. Where at the end he could join the adult world, claim the shared experience that everyone else found so easy to acquire. Then he wouldn't have that word in his head all the time: I'm thirty-eight and a *virgin*. Approaching the age of the man in that movie he'd hoped wouldn't get as popular as it had. But that doesn't matter now. After today, he'll be just thirty-eight and anyone.

By now it's dark outside, the room lit by tea lights set up in rows on every surface. The keystone candle is shaped like a woman. The light from her flame brightens her bulbous body from hip to neck, and her powerful posture thrills him. He digs his toes into the carpet, hanging on in case the room tips upside down.

"Feeling more confident?" Sarah-Beth asks.

With a rush of gratitude, he drops his robe. June covers her mouth. The AC breathes on Martin's skin, chilling parts of his body that stiff, corporate air has never touched.

"I guess he's into it," Sarah-Beth says. June braces herself against the wicker.

He steps toward Kate. She blinks and offers a steady, effortful look. He feels himself hardening, though he's too nervous to look down, afraid of how his penis must appear, twitching like a whisker between his legs as he edges toward her. He rarely walks around in the nude. He always changes clothes in one spot on the rug, sinking footprints into the pile. He wears a towel into and out of the bathroom, even when no one's home.

Kate's breath is dark, sweet bread. He'd planned to stroke her, to slip off her clothes, to behave like a burst of joy, but his hands are too active, beyond his control. He pulls her sweater over her head. Her face catches in the neckline.

"Ow," she says.

Sarah-Beth giggles, and Kate rubs her nose.

"Sorry," Martin says. "Are you okay? I'm so sorry."

She takes off the rest of her clothes herself. Her nipples are knobby, like buttons. He presses them, but his fingers are dry. He'd lick them, but maybe that's too much. She stares at the ceiling like it's giving her instructions. This whole process is so awkward that he just wants to finish. He doesn't know why he ever thought having sex in front of an audience of strangers would be erotic.

He cups his hands over Kate's kneecaps. Her muscles are tight. She must be nervous. He pets her, and her legs fall apart. He spits on his hands and rubs himself. That brings him back to life, and he wants to close his eyes against the scene, tip his head back, and keep touching himself. For the first time in thirty-eight years, he's moving toward the opening of a woman, and he's staying firm. The realization shrinks him, and he strokes once more before pushing in.

Once inside, he's as still as a rabbit in the grass. The sensation is so overwhelming, all that damp skin forcing against him, that he doesn't have to move. But he remembers "quickly and with gratitude," and pumps.

He looks around during the process. June's skin has been imprinted with the wicker, like she's pressing so deeply into the chair that it's absorbing her. Sarah-Beth's smile is frozen: she's not laughing anymore. Winnie watches with an expression he can't read, eyebrows together, mouth flat. She looks like she wants to say something, but can't yet. This act seems like it could never heal anyone, like it's boring for the girls, at best. At worst, he doesn't want to imagine. He feels sorry for Winnie, with all her careful sessions and supplements.

Martin expects the scene to end fast, like Winnie wanted. He's a virgin, after all. But he keeps going, in and out, and it's taking forever, pleasure sliding away the harder he seeks it. At a certain point he remembers what Winnie said about what the girls have been through and he wants to pull out, but that's not what she said was best for them, so he reaches a hand around and pats Kate on the back. *This is comforting*, he telegraphs to her. *I'm a comforting member of your sex community*. She looks at him for the first time, and frowns.

After what feels like half an hour, she isn't any more into the act than she was when they started, and Martin remembers what Sarah-Beth said. Kate does look bored.

Her hair is bushy, free, and loose. He clasps a handful on either side of her face, giving her a chance to react. When she doesn't, he tugs, harder than planned.

LYDIA CONKLIN

Kate gasps and he spasms. The two functions happen simultaneously, like the reaction of one organism. Stunned, he pulls out, wipes himself on the robe, and rolls back onto his heels.

His head clears. He did it. Maybe he didn't satisfy Kate, whose eyelids sink as though she were powering down her brain, but he showed himself to have endurance, at least. And he didn't chicken out or go soft. That counts for something.

He remembers he's supposed to be grateful, so he says, "Thank you very much," like an awkward Elvis. He wants to hug her, but he's taken too long already. How long is twenty-five minutes?

Sarah-Beth helps Kate get dressed, murmuring in her ear. They leave with June trailing them, hands over her face. Martin is confused. Suddenly he's alone with Winnie. His nakedness tingles, so he pulls his robe onto his lap. She sits next to him on the carpet.

"Honey," she says. "It's been a hard couple days."

"I guess." The rats have left scratches on his shoulders and neck. But Winnie doesn't know that. And nothing else was bad. What just happened—it wasn't great, maybe, but it could've been worse. He's even a little proud.

Winnie thumps the rat scratches too hard. He disguises his anguish with a friendly grimace.

"I should have been more specific with my instructions," she says. "But you'll do better next time. Usually virgins are different."

"How?" he asks, his voice a peep.

"Grateful," she says. "Into it. Quick. Simple."

He thought he'd be like that, but how could he control it? His hurt must show, because she says, "Oh, honey," and hugs him, folding him into her smell, which is like bubble gum even though she isn't chewing any. She holds him for so long that Martin forgets where he is. His body relaxes. He swears hers does, too, muscles slackening.

There's a wiggle and the robe slides off his lap. Then her pants are down and she's pulled him on top of her.

"Kiss me first," she says.

He kisses like he always kisses, his mouth fitting over the border of her lips so he can contain her mouth in his. She nibbles at him, folds down his aperture, guiding him to a slit. She herds his tongue away, tapping it with her own each time he strokes her teeth or flicks the back of her throat.

She moans. He can't believe that the glowing knots of her cheekbones, her regal nose, are this close.

"Much better," she says. "Now." She takes his hand and glides it under her shirt. He snatches her breast the moment his fingertips reach its boundary, but she pries them loose, guides them gingerly along the swell. She makes him touch her for a long time, and a funny thing happens where Martin becomes a combination of relaxed and even more excited than before. Like his body winds up to spite itself. He's pushing against her leg. He can't help it.

"Okay, tiger." She guides him in and then they're rocking on the floor.

He doesn't take as long this time. And he swears there's a loosening in the sharp line of her jaw; her eyes shimmer in a way they never do at the communal dinners, when she sits at the head of the table, alone, monitoring, never sharing herself.

When he finishes, she beams. "Now we're getting somewhere."

He dons his robe quickly, preserving the moment, and hurries upstairs.

*   *   *

Back safe in his room, he opens the door to his closet and sniffs. All he smells is leather. Two rats must be too few to stink. He reaches into the cowboy boot and pulls out the animals.

They sit still on his hand, nostrils pulsing. Usually they skitter all over him, trying to crawl upside down along the bottom of his wrist, up his forearm, and across his chest. But sometimes, very rarely and only at the beginning of a session, they'll sit quietly. Though they're merely disoriented from being removed into a bright environment, he likes to think they're at peace. Enjoying human contact for a rare moment. Relaxing.

He brings the rats to his nose. One stretches its muzzle all the way to his skin. The whiskers tickle.

Though the next day is Friday, not the day of the Community Sex Act, at breakfast Winnie asks Martin to come by her room after work.

All day at the office, Martin struggles over the source code he's testing. He pictures entering that white bedroom and facing the girls. Now that Winnie has trained him, maybe they're eager for a second attempt, an extra Sex Act on a Friday. He pictures Sarah-Beth's sly mouth, Kate's quick breath. Maybe he should try a different girl this time. He couldn't gather enough nerve for Sarah-Beth, though, and he doesn't want to frighten June. He's not looking forward to her turn, because, though she's older than him, she's as disengaged as a teenager. He could go for Winnie, but he couldn't perform in front of everyone like he did last night. And it wouldn't be right. The Starlight is a commune, but his relationship with Winnie is separate.

Carla approaches, handing back reports to engineers, dodging small talk in an artful way Martin can never manage. She reads novels at her desk, leaning back with the book propped in front of her, her face relaxed in pleasure, the way Hannah Bernhardt probably does, wherever she has a job now. Carla saves up time for this practice by performing efficiently throughout the day. Even though her hair is frizzy and she doesn't dye the gray out, even though she has only two work outfits that are both brown suits, and even though her glasses are crooked on her nose, she's only twenty-nine, with the exact same wise, golden baby face as Hannah Bernhardt—which stills Martin's breath every time she turns her attention on him—and she owns the most elegant earrings. Today she wears teal stones wrapped in copper wire. The earrings are heavy but sit comfortably inserted, without distortion to the flesh. He's startled that she wants to talk to him, and he looks over his shoulder even though his desk is in a corner.

"How many you got these days?" she asks.

For one horrifying second Martin thinks she means women. But then he remembers. "Just two." He's proud to say it. Two rats is normal. Not excessive at all.

But Carla looks aghast. "Oh god. What happened?"

Martin freezes. "They got sick?"

Carla retreats, hugging a file folder to her chest. "Like the plague or what?"

He should've just said he moved. He tries to remember the last time he mentioned the rats, and how many he had then. They started with six, only one male, so he must've admitted to at least that many. He's pretty sure he reported to her after the first four litters, because that was when they bought the second tank. He might've told her about the third tank, too, because somewhere along the way she got the idea that the population was growing at a notable rate. So that's a hefty number of deaths on his hands. He doesn't even know how he'd dispose of so many bodies. You couldn't flush them.

"It's a sad time," he says.

Carla looks at him the way Hannah Bernhardt looked at him years ago, scooting away from him across her sunflower duvet the moment he pulled down his underwear. "But it's not like that with us," Hannah said. "Martin. We're above that." He breathed through his nose as he nodded, the back of his mind a dark explosion. She gave him a stack of nineteenth-century novels, which illustrated, she said, a pace of romance more amenable to her disposition: languorous, with melancholy flavoring passion. But he hadn't been smart enough to get through more than twenty pages of *Wuthering Heights*. The failure shamed him. When she asked about the book, he mumbled nonsense and her shoulders slumped.

Confronting Hannah's same baby face on Carla now, he feels like an asshole twice over. A guy who's had dozens of pets die in a few days' time and illustrates the experience with a shrug. He opens his mouth. Acid sears his throat.

"Excuse me," he says, bowing his head to his monitor. "I have to finish up."

That evening Martin visits Winnie's room wearing his cloth robe. He passes the sign in the hallway suggesting FRUITFUL OPENINGS FOR HEALTHY CONVERSATION. He's tried every one—A FOND CHILDHOOD MEMORY; A TIME YOU WERE IN CHARGE—but none led to much. Winnie's door is ajar. She stands in her outfit from the law firm where she works as a paralegal: a pencil skirt and an untucked silk blouse. She has the best job of all the girls at the Starlight. Everyone else is a waitress or checkout clerk. She's talking to June, whose back is curved away.

"One more try," Winnie says. "Please, Junie. Forget the silly meals. Ignore the placards if they bother you. Those are just for fun."

"How is any of this in any way 'fun'?"

Winnie sighs with her whole body. "Not fun,

okay? But it does actually help if you buy the whole program. It's about faith, even in the silly stuff."

"That's so churchy."

"I know you laugh about my booklets and herbal treatments and whatever," Winnie says. "And the Sex Act, probably, too. All you girls do. And, right, sure. I get it. You think I'm stupid?"

"No."

"But if you can bear to suspend your cynicism, that's when you'll get somewhere." She flaps her hand at a shelf above her bed containing packets and baskets and tinctures, all in soft, nonthreatening shades of rose and lilac and coral, so neatly arranged, so dustless, they must be tended to regularly. "Think of it like a costume." Winnie straightens her back. "Like the cops I worked with back in the day. A bunch of tools put on polyester shirts and are invested with all this disgusting power."

"I hate costume parties. And I hate cops."

Winnie lifts her hands. "I'm with you, Junie. Trust me." But she doesn't sound like she's with June. She sounds like she cares, sure, but the way she talks is stiff, rehearsed. June isn't even looking at her. "Talk to the other girls. They all felt the same way, in the beginning."

"But it's not the beginning for me. I'm forty-three."

Martin eases the door wider, while staying recessed in the shadows. Winnie takes June's arm. June thrusts her away like she's been seared.

"I just can't stand it," says June.

"I know, I know," pleads Winnie. "That's why we're here."

June brushes past Martin without even registering him. "Hi, June," he calls, so Winnie can see he's trying to be friends, not eavesdrop.

"Oh, Martin." Winnie straightens herself. "You didn't need to wear that." She wrinkles her nose into a dried mushroom.

"It's comfortable," he says.

"I only wanted to ask a computer question."

His shoulders wilt. Civilians ask him about computers all the time. That's inevitable in his field. They ask about jammed printers, broken monitor casings, water damage, even though he's a software guy. People befriend him just for tech support. After yesterday, he'd hoped he and Winnie would have more urgent matters to discuss.

But of course he'll help. Despite his grumblings, he savors erasing panic. He sits down, and she cracks open her laptop. She's struggling with a program, so at least she's gotten his field right. He doesn't recognize the blue sun icon.

"Do you have the original disk?"

"I got it online," she says. "For free."

"This should be easy, then."

Her cheeks brighten. "Really?"

Martin tries not to smile. He loves the tone people adopt when he helps them with computers. It's the liveliest anyone ever acts in front of him.

"I've been fussing with it all day."

Martin shakes his head. Though any American spends an average of four recreational hours on the computer daily, most don't know how to perform even the simplest maintenance. He deletes the old copy and reinstalls.

"See?" he says. "You probably got a buggy version. Or they've made fixes."

"Wow," Winnie says. "This is fabulous."

She opens the program and her screen fills with sky. Not a cartoon sky, but a sky composed of complicated blues, a sky with depth and motion. She populates the air with artfully detailed birds and bugs and helicopters selected from a sidebar. Once released, the figures float and flap in randomized patterns. When figures meet, an interaction occurs. A bird swallows a bug. A jet pops a balloon. A dragon barbecues a parachute. Martin is lulled, watching the screen.

"There's no point to it," Winnie says. "I know it's stupid. But the sun sets in real time. Then you can do, like, bats and stuff. And restless, winged businessmen."

Martin is often puzzled by the programs that absorb people. But there's something about the design of this one. The colors are creamy, the figures invested, somehow, with a core of life. Winnie has taste.

A pterodactyl crashes into a Pegasus. A chickadee disappears inside the engine of an Airbus. A flying squirrel rides a drone. Winnie melts with giggles. Martin has never seen her so goofy and free.

"It's all I can handle after work and the co-op."

Her shoulders hunch. "It's the only time I forget the point of me."

"You're doing important work," Martin says.

"Well. Once you start."

"Really, though. I mean it."

She throws her arms around him. He holds his breath. She adjusts her body, bearing down on his crotch, then pulls back far enough to see him. He can't get used to her this close; so much dignified elegance inches away sets his face on fire. He's reminded of a trick he tried as a kid when he was lonely. He'd press his nose against a face in a magazine. If he looked closely enough, crossing his eyes, he could pretend the model was lying on the table before him.

This time there are no lessons. Winnie doesn't adjust Martin's kissing, and he slips into his old ways. He loves that feeling of containing another mouth inside his own. And she doesn't sputter or gag like other girls he's been with. She tips her head back and takes it.

Afterward, they lie on the rug, holding each other around Winnie's crumpled blouse and Martin's robe. Each topic Martin thinks of seems wrong. He can't ask if this is a lesson, because it's clearly not. He can't ask if the other girls would be jealous if they knew. He can't discuss the next Community Sex Act, and what he should do to improve, because that would be fatally unromantic. Instead he asks, "Why don't you allow pets?," though that's the worst topic of all.

She shakes her head, loose and easy on her neck. "We're about human connections here. Substitutes make recovery harder. Like alcoholics and candy."

"But people can have pets and human relationships." Not that he'd ever managed the latter.

"It's good for us to limit the focal points. Our girls already have so much to manage."

"Oh." Kate had said she liked the comfort of dogs. He pictures a fluffy fox skittering around the commune, leaping from lap to lap. How could it bring anything but joy?

"Why?" she asks. "Are you a pet person?"

Martin shakes his head, a tight, small gesture that could be second-guessed later.

"You're trying with us, Martin. I appreciate that."

He can't believe those fingers playing with the fuzz along her chin, that foot curling under her thigh, all the flesh between, engaged with him. He can't believe that someone this attractive—more than that, someone this put-together—would want to sleep with him. What a shame it would be to let the rats go. Their private, scrabbling visits are the highlight of his day. But he longs to do this right.

That evening, he zips the rats into his panniers with a handful of shavings and food pellets. He grinds his teeth as he drops them in, but he reminds himself of Winnie, her soft skin and warmth all over him, and he mounts his Bianchi, passing Sarah-Beth, stationed on the stoop with a lemonade, head back, so blissed-out she doesn't see him.

And then he's off. Away from the co-op. Through the wild fennel and papery, unstable eucalyptus trees, he finds the bike path, passing a preschool with a formal shield on its sign like a junior branch of the Ivy League and a spay-and-neuter clinic whose clouds of bougainvillea soften the howls inside. He leans his bike against a cypress, the trunk bowing under the weight of the aluminum. He takes the rats out and holds them to his face. Then he sets them down on the path.

He begs them to run the instant they hit the thirsty earth, so he'll have no chance for second thoughts. They're animals. They must long to be free. He feels awful, but he has to do this. And maybe Winnie is right. Maybe the rats have distracted him from seeking human companionship.

But they just sit there in the dust, a spill of gray-brown fuzz. Wind wrinkles the fluff on their humped backs. One climbs onto his shoe, tastes his laces, then races up his leg to his groin.

At brunch the next day, Martin chatters pleasantly. He's energized by his reclamation of the rats and his extracurricular session with Winnie. June stirs her food until the kale and tofu steak and fava beans are a gluey mash. She studies the sticky lump as though a message might bubble out. Winnie asks Martin questions about work, with bright, encouraging eyes.

"What a cheerful group we are," Sarah-Beth says, interrupting Martin's account of a policy meeting. "Anyone else missing the good old nightlife?"

"No," says Kate.

"We could be out there pumping whiskies," Sarah-Beth says, cementing tofu slices together with mustard. "Checking out dudes. Bitching about our shitty-ass jobs. How about it?"

"That could be a relaxing way to spend an evening," Martin says, checking on Winnie from the corner of his eye.

"You'll get there," Winnie says.

Color rises in June's cheeks, so much impacted hope.

"I don't know about that," Kate says. "Considering."

June snaps her head around to Kate. "What do you mean?"

"I'd like to discuss my personal experience of this week's Community Sex Act," Kate says, glancing at Sarah-Beth.

Martin sets down his speared kale and sits up straight. He wasn't expecting Kate to relate her personal reactions in front of him. Shouldn't she save it for the Sharing Meetings? She wasn't even looking at him.

"Tell us everything," says Sarah-Beth, eyes sparkling.

"Well." Kate looks around the table. "The 'person in question' basically walked into the room. Smelling like a Band-Aid from his day at work."

The one time Martin had tried to engage Kate in friendship, he'd recounted a childhood memory of watching other boys play on his street. That day they hadn't chased him away, just let him watch as they traced graceful patterns across the blacktop, kicking rubber pucks and shouting, blocking one another with complex, light-footed choreography. His skin had tingled when they got close, thinking that maybe, in the next round, he could join.

"And?" Sarah-Beth asks, as though Kate needed encouragement.

"He dropped his clothes and stood there, dick wagging."

"Gross."

"Yeah. It was like he wanted me to do something. Like he thought he was some prize."

"Ew."

"I know, right? As though I can't get any guy I want."

"So then what happened?"

"He fucked me." She's fighting tears now, fingers tight on the rim of the table. "He didn't even kiss me. Just in and out."

"He didn't touch you?"

"Maybe he pinched my nipple, like, once."

"God."

Martin drops his fork, which hits the table, spraying crumbs. He felt good after the Community Sex Act. Sure, Winnie corrected him. But he thought he'd done all right. He wants to push his chair back and flee the room, but Winnie told him to be easy. He straightens his shoulders and tries to look open and kind. But his forehead burns.

"I'm sorry to hear that," he says, voice trembling. "You've probably noticed that I'm not the smoothest person."

"I have a double today," Kate says, standing. Now she'll go serve people for fourteen hours, in some ratty apron, dull-eyed and listless, ordered from table to table by alpha customers and alpha bosses and uncaring waitress peers. He wants to urge her to stay, so they can talk about it, so he can do better down the road. But she won't look at him.

Kate, June, and Sarah-Beth leave as soon as Winnie goes to the kitchen for the vegan Boston cream pie. When she returns with the pie in her hands, she stalls in the doorway, her sinking face reflected in the plasticky dark fudge.

"Where are they," she asks, voice flat.

"I think they went to work?" He can't stand for her to look any sadder than this.

"They left, didn't they?" She sets the cake down so hard the fudge wobbles. "They all left." She collapses into her seat.

"I'm sure the others will be back."

"But not Kate." Winnie balances her forehead on her hand. The tips of her hair trace contours in the fudge. "We were getting somewhere. I was doing a good job." Her words are tense, like she might scream.

"You did do a good job," Martin says. "You were wonderful." His voice is shaky. "Winnie, have some cake."

"I'm sorry." She takes a breath, sits up straighter.

"Here I am, having my own meltdown, when it's you I should worry about."

At this Martin freezes. He waits for her to continue, watching closely. Winnie takes her time, pushing her hair behind her ears, the strands fudge-tipped.

"It looks bad now," she says, "we feel bad, but we have to remember." She fills her lungs. "Toxicity is part of healing." She says the words like a mantra, like she's trying to convince herself. "That energy is hard to receive. You did well, Martin. I know Kate's comments didn't feel good. But they're not bad girls. We have to remember that. We have to be patient." She lifts out a wedge of cake like it's lead, fatigue dragging down her face.

His throat clenched during Kate's story, fever in his cheeks. He wasn't great at sex, but it had been his first time, and all those eyes were on him. He feels proud of himself for receiving her energy so well, like Winnie said.

"I told you these girls have tricky pasts. They deserve to begin again with someone easy. Someone old enough to be respectful, who's grateful for whatever they can provide. Then they can start to

feel good again. I've seen it work out many times."
She studies him. "Your failing, honey, is that your
heart's too young."

"Sorry," Martin says. But the back of his neck
prickles. He doesn't see how that—or any of it—is
his fault.

"The problem is—" She sighs. "The problem is,
we ruin guys sometimes."

A bitter hiccup pops in his throat. "Yeah."

"I'm sorry. It's not our intention."

"I get it." He leans over, seizing his gut. Kale
slurry mercilessly churns.

"You're a solid guy. But you can't be hard on our
girls. They've been through a lot. Listen. I shouldn't
tell you this, but Kate especially. That's why she's
been here so long." She gazes at the door. "After her
Inciting Trauma, she couldn't go back to work. She
was a plastics engineer. Really high up. Even after
her hair grew back, she couldn't bear to go in."

Numbers and designs, squashed from Kate's
brain by some nightmare Martin can't imagine.
Couldn't even begin to imagine. Doesn't deserve to
try. "But that's awful." How could Winnie let him
bungle around with someone who'd seen trauma

like that? How could he not have taken seriously his responsibility? He'd tried to be a burst of joy. But he hadn't really believed, had secretly found Winnie's doodads goofy, the Sex Act frivolous. He'd never imagined a girl leaping up from his body after sex, well-adjusted and loving men. He's sickened by how he mechanically inserted himself, not even bothering to kiss Kate or touch her or use lube. And he'd actually jerked her hair.

"It will be all right." Winnie looks down. "Maybe she'll come back. Some of them do." She turns to the window, which frames the burrito shop, its glowing neon tortilla blinking with a broken tube. "It's not your fault," she says, without conviction.

Years ago, when Martin told his best friend, Jerry, about Hannah Bernhardt freaking out when he'd initiated sex, Jerry had said she must've been traumatized before; that he'd heard a rumor, actually, about some dark time with a cousin. Martin had never known whether to believe Jerry or whether he was just trying to make Martin feel better. He'd been too young, too stupid, to ask Hannah. He still doesn't know whether he should have.

Winnie stands. Martin thought they were at the beginning of their evening. He can't be alone. He needs Winnie's understanding, her terms and exercises, her new age magic that at least promises explanation. He needs her to know, too, that the Starlight is working.

He seizes the fringe of her skirt.

She turns. "What are you doing?" Her voice is sharp.

The fabric slides from his grip. "I thought we could, I don't know."

"Martin," she says. "Please. Control yourself."

Her tone pricks him in the heart. Martin draws his arm into his lap and looks away, focusing on a vein of kale on the floor tiles, until Winnie has shut herself back in her room.

Martin knocks on Winnie's door, but she doesn't answer. She's put out a sign asserting that PRIVACY CAN BE REQUESTED AT ANY INTERVAL. Behind the door is her ragged breath. He couldn't bear to see her, anyway.

In his room, Martin frees the rats. He lies on the floor and they run over him. They dedicate their attention to different quadrants of his body, sniffing and scrabbling, reminding him of each of his features, returning him to himself. He loves Winnie. The first time he saw her in the coffee shop, her head was a balloon floating over the steam, that stately, tired face the only one that mattered. And now their connection has been lost.

A darkness lands on his head, heavy as a damp towel. He's made Kate start over, all due to his own selfishness. He can't believe he's not a virgin anymore. Because even though virginity was so embarrassing, even though he tried to hide it from Clive through the years they lived together, even though every time he came close to sleeping with a girl he was afraid she'd run from the room screaming to the world that Martin Lordlawn was a virgin, at least being a virgin made Martin feel like he'd kept a part of himself that everyone else had given away. When he saw kids on the street, he thought: You're so young and already you've traded your fresh eyes for a perspective that might not be better.

And maybe his virginity had made him more sensitive, more careful. Maybe, though his dates never knew he was a virgin, his virginity had drawn them to him, his excitement and innocence. Carla waves hello to him every day.

More than all that, when he was a virgin, he couldn't hurt anyone. He'd always known the loss of his virginity would mean pain, for himself and others. He'd avoided that pain above everything. And now here it was. He'd gotten what he wanted, and he'd flattened someone along the way. He was probably never meant to have sex at all.

On Monday at work, Carla lingers during lunch, standing by her desk and thumbing a book so thick Martin can't imagine holding it aloft to read. She's skirted his desk ever since she heard about the rats, applying hand sanitizer anytime he came near, but today he spots her in the boundary of his vision. The rest of the office is at a restaurant. Maybe she chose this moment so no one would see her attempt to catch his attention.

He calls her over, standing up and holding himself steady. She looks up, startled as a fawn.

He takes a breath. Winnie last night, telling him he was ruined. He doesn't want it to be true. "Do you like me?"

Carla's mouth screws up like she's tasted something sour. She forces a smile, the one she uses to dodge small talk. "You're a nice guy, Martin."

Martin deflates. But she does like him, he's sure. "Would you have a date with me?" How wonderful to invite Hannah Bernhardt's face out for the slow courtship she always deserved, to end the story the way it should've ended decades ago.

"Well," she says, "I guess, maybe, sometime." She looks down at her book.

He steps back. Carla would date him, he can see that. Once, to be polite, maybe more, so as not to hurt or anger him. She wears Winnie's face from their practice sessions, which he now suspects was only a professional expression of pleasure, just enough color in her cheeks to keep him going. Shame burns his ears: pressing Carla would only be selfish, the way joining the Starlight was selfish, the way his Sex Act was selfish, and keeping the rats and messing with Kate and barely cracking Hannah's novels. He wants to be a good guy, but he's not. The nicest thing he can do is let Carla go. "That's all right," he says. "It's nice just to work together."

She gives him a real smile, and he nearly manages one in reply. Has he done the right thing this time, finally? He leans over the industrial carpet between them, peering at the glassy finish of her expression, seeking salvation in her relief.

And then, as he leans closer, she steps away with a hot blip of fear. A thrill runs down the crest of his back.

From 2011 to 2014, PHAEDRA CHARLES was senior designer at Louise Fili Ltd, and from 2015 to 2019 she was a partner at Charles&Thorn, a boutique typographic and illustration studio. In 2014, she was part of the class of ADC Young Guns 12. She has taught at the School of Visual Arts in New York City, is a graduate of the Type@ Cooper Extended Program at the Cooper Union, and served as communication judge for the Type Directors Club 2017 annual. From 2018 to 2020, she developed and led a variable font project, Fraunces, with support from Google Fonts. Currently, she runs Undercase Type and is a brand designer for Gander.

ANELISE CHEN is the author of the novel *So Many Olympic Exertions*.

JOHN LEE CLARK is the author, most recently, of *How to Communicate*. His essay "Against Access," which appeared in *McSweeney's Quarterly* 64, was the 2022 winner of the Krause Essay Prize. A DeafBlind educator, he travels extensively to teach Protactile. He makes his home in St. Paul, Minnesota, with artist Adrean Clark and their three kids and two cats.

LYDIA CONKLIN has received a Stegner Fellowship in fiction at Stanford University, a Rona Jaffe Foundation Writers' Award, three Pushcart Prizes, a Fulbright grant in creative writing in Poland, a grant from the

Elizabeth George Foundation, and fellowships from Emory University, MacDowell, Yaddo, Hedgebrook, and elsewhere. Their fiction has appeared in *Tin House*, *American Short Fiction*, the *Paris Review*, *One Story*, and *Virginia Quarterly Review*. They are an assistant professor of fiction at Vanderbilt University. Their story collection, *Rainbow Rainbow*, was published by Catapult.

YOHANCA DELGADO is a 2021–23 Wallace Stegner Fellow in fiction at Stanford University and a 2022 National Endowment for the Arts Creative Writing Fellow. Her recent fiction has appeared in the *Paris Review*, *One Story*, *A Public Space*, and *Zyzzyva*. Her stories have been anthologized in *The Best Short Stories 2022: The O. Henry Prize Winners*, *The Best American Short Stories 2022*, and *The Best American Science Fiction and Fantasy 2021*.

MAX DELSOHN's writing appears in *VICE*, the *Rumpus*, *Triangle House*, *Nat. Brut*, and *Passages North*, among other places. They are an MFA candidate in fiction at Syracuse University. They are currently working on a short-story collection and a novel.

JACKIE FERRENTINO is an illustrator currently based in Brooklyn, New York.

BIANCA GIAEVER is a radio producer and filmmaker in New York City. She is the creator and host of the world's most slowly and lovingly produced podcast, *Constellation Prize*.

JULIE HECHT is the author of *Do the Windows Open?*, a collection of nine stories, all first published in the *New Yorker*. She is also the author of the story collection *Happy Trails to You*, the novel *The Unprofessionals*, and the nonfiction book, *Was This Man a Genius?: Talks with Andy Kaufman*. She is writing her next book, *Every Single Thing*. This is her third story to appear in *McSweeney's Quarterly*.

SOPHIE HUGHES translates Spanish and Latin American writers such as Alia Trabucco Zerán and Enrique Vila-Matas. In 2021 she was awarded the Queen Sofía Spanish Institute Translation Prize for Fernanda Melchor's *Hurricane Season*.

EVAN JAMES is the author of *Cheer Up, Mr. Widdicombe* and *I've Been Wrong Before*. He lives in Brooklyn, New York.

RICARDO FRASSO JARAMILLO is a poet and writer whose work has been published in the *New York Times*, the *Believer*, the *Rumpus*, and elsewhere. He is a 2022–23 National Book Critics Circle Emerging Critics Fellow, as well as a case manager at a high school for immigrant youth in the Oakland Unified School District.

MEL KASSEL's short stories have appeared in *The Best American Science Fiction and Fantasy 2021*, *Black Warrior Review*, and elsewhere. She is a graduate of the Iowa Writers' Workshop and a World Fantasy Award winner. Despite being a dog person who loves the ocean, she lives in the Midwest with a big gray cat.

APRIL AYERS LAWSON is the author of *Virgin and Other Stories* and winner of the 2011 Plimpton Prize for Fiction. Her writing has appeared in *Granta*, *Der Spiegel*, the *Paris Review*, and elsewhere.

SIQI LIU is a writer from Changsha, China, and Naperville, Illinois. Her work has appeared in *The Pushcart Prize XLV: Best of the Small Presses 2021* anthology and the *Harvard Advocate*. She is currently getting an MFA in fiction at the Iowa Writers' Workshop.

BENJAMIN MARRA is the cartoonist behind the comic books *Night Business*, *American Blood*, *Disciples*, and *Terror Assaulter: O.M.W.O.T. (One Man War on Terror)*. His illustration for Numero Group's album *Wayfaring Strangers: Acid Nightmares* garnered him a Grammy nomination. Acclaimed comic book writer Grant Morrison selected Marra as a collaborator for his first issue editing the seminal comic book magazine *Heavy Metal*. Marra's work has been recognized by the Society of Illustrators, the Society of Publication Designers, and American Illustration. He lives in Montreal.

FERNANDA MELCHOR is widely recognized as "one of Mexico's most exciting new voices" (*Guardian*). She won the Anna Seghers Prize and the International Literature Award for *Hurricane Season*, which was also longlisted for the National Book Award for Translated Literature, shortlisted for the International Booker Prize, and was a *New York Times* Notable Book. Her latest novel is *Paradais*.

LEILA RENEE earned her MFA in creative writing from Syracuse University. She received the 2021 Gulf Coast Prize in Fiction and the 2022 Shirley Jackson Prize in Fiction from Syracuse University. Her work has appeared in *Prairie Schooner,* Harvard University's *Transition Magazine*, *Gulf Coast*, *Columbia Journal*, *Electric Literature*, the *Offing*, *Split Lip Magazine*, and other publications. She is the visiting assistant professor of creative writing at Pacific Lutheran University.

MIKKEL ROSENGAARD is the author of *The Invention of Ana*. His stories have been published in five languages and have appeared in *Bookforum*, *BOMB* magazine, *Guernica*, and elsewhere. He is a MacDowell Fellow and a recipient of the Danish Art Foundation's Young Artistic Elite Fellowship. He grew up in Elsinore, Denmark, and lives in New York City.

IKECHUKWU UFOMADU is an Emmy Award–nominated actor, writer, and comedian and was named one of "Five NYC Comedians to Look Out For in 2018" by *Time Out New York*. He cowrote and stars in the short-form series *Words with Ike* and the indie feature *Inspector Ike*. He currently writes for the late-night show *Ziwe* and was an inaugural recipient of the Jerome Hill Artist Fellowship.

ZACH WILLIAMS is a 2021–23 Wallace Stegner Fellow in fiction at Stanford University. His work has appeared in the *New Yorker* and the *Paris Review*.

CONNOR WILLUMSEN is an award-winning Canadian cartoonist and visual artist whose books *Anti-Gone* and *Bradley of Him* have received wide acclaim in multiple languages. *Anti-Gone* was subsequently adapted into a mixed-reality performance by the artist Theo Triantafyllidis. He has been featured in notable comics anthologies such as *Kramers Ergot* and *Best American Comics*.

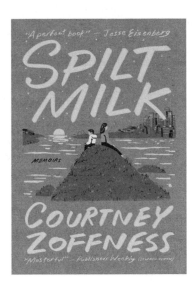

SPILT MILK
by Courtney Zoffness

What role does a mother play in raising thoughtful, generous children? Internationally award-winning writer Courtney Zoffness considers what we inherit from generations past—biologically, culturally, spiritually—and what we pass on to our children. *Spilt Milk* is an intimate, bracing, and beautiful exploration of vulnerability and culpability. Zoffness relives her childhood anxiety disorder as she witnesses it manifesting in her firstborn; endures brazen sexual advances from a student in her class; grapples with the implications of her young son's cop obsession; and challenges her Jewish faith. Where is the line between privacy and secrecy? How do the stories we tell inform who we become? These powerful, dynamic essays herald a vital new voice.

McSWEENEY'S 64: THE AUDIO ISSUE

Combining art, fiction, audio, and over a dozen unclassifiable print objects in a custom box, *McSweeney's 64* is a riotous exploration of audiovisual storytelling, coproduced with Radiotopia from PRX. Included are Rion Amilcar Scott, with a short fiction piece featuring two alternative audio endings; Pulitzer Prize–nominated composer Kate Soper, with a transhumanist, interactive software upload; DeafBlind poet John Lee Clark on the limits of accessibility; Aliya Pabani, with a radio drama whose plot is complicated by a 24" × 30" illustrated poster; Ian Chillag, with an absurdist, interactive phone tree; James T. Green, Catherine Lacey, and *This American Life*'s Sean Cole, with voicemail dispatches to the editor; Kali Fajardo-Anstine, Aimee Bender, and Kelli Jo Ford, with short stories that braid in audio; and so much more.

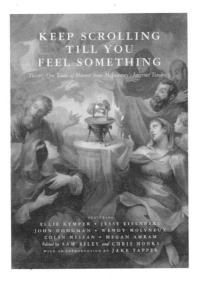

KEEP SCROLLING TILL YOU FEEL SOMETHING
edited by Sam Riley and Chris Monks

It's a great undertaking to raise a humor website from infancy to full-fledged adulthood, but with the right editors, impeccable taste, and a dire political landscape, your site will enjoy years of relevance and comic validation. Join us as we revisit the first twenty-one years of McSweeney's Internet Tendency, from our bright-eyed and bewildered early stages to our world-weary and bewildered recent days. *Keep Scrolling Till You Feel Something* is a coming-of-age celebration of the pioneering website, featuring brand-new pieces and classics by some of today's best humor writers, like Ellie Kemper, Wendy Molyneux, Jesse Eisenberg, Karen Chee, Colin Nissan, John Moe, and many more.

ALSO AVAILABLE
FROM McSWEENEY'S

FICTION

POETRY

COLLINS LIBRARY

ALL THIS AND MORE AT

store.mcsweeneys.net

Founded in 1998, McSweeney's is an independent publisher based in San Francisco. McSweeney's exists to champion ambitious and inspired new writing, and to challenge conventional expectations about where it's found, how it looks, and who participates. We're here to discover things we love, help them find their most resplendent form, and place them into the hands of curious, engaged readers.

THERE ARE SEVERAL WAYS TO SUPPORT MCSWEENEY'S:

Support Us on Patreon
visit *www.patreon.com/mcsweeneysinternettendency*

Subscribe & Shop
visit *store.mcsweeneys.net*

Volunteer & Intern
email *contact@mcsweeneys.net*

Sponsor Books & *Quarterlies*
email *amanda@mcsweeneys.net*

To learn more, please visit *www.mcsweeneys.net/donate*
or contact Executive Director Amanda Uhle at
amanda@mcsweeneys.net or 415.642.5609.

McSweeney's Literary Arts Fund is a nonprofit
organization as described by IRS 501(c)(3).
Your support is invaluable to us.